1

Dead Ringer

A Play

Charles Ross

Adapted from *The Prime Pretender by*
Logan Gourlay

Samuel French – London
New York – Sydney – Toronto – Hollywood

DEAD RINGER

First performed at the Thorndike Theatre, Leatherhead
on 8th February, 1983, with Hugh Hastings as Ray
Turnbull.

Subsequently presented by Bill Kenwright and Charles
Ross at the Duke of York's Theatre, London, on 17th
May, 1983, with the following cast:

Randolph Bolton	William Franklyn
Frances Cowdray	Patricia Lawrence
Dick Marr	Basil Moss
Nigel Haywood	Adrian King
Ray Turnbull	McDonald Hobley
Gerry Jackson	William Franklyn
Eva Bolton	Sylvia Syms
Colonel Hardacre	Geoffrey Colville

The play directed by Roger Clissold
Designed by Stuart Stanley

The action takes place in the study of the Prime Minister
at Number 10 Downing Street, Westminster. The time is
in the not too distant future.

ACT I   SCENE 1 Late at night
          SCENE 2 Three days later. Late afternoon

ACT II SCENE 1 Immediately following
          SCENE 2 Three weeks later

The photograph on p. iv is by Phil Whittington and shows the Thorndike
Theatre set

ACT I

SCENE 1

The Prime Minister's study at Number 10, Downing Street. The time is the reasonably near future

It is late at night and the chimes of Big Ben are heard striking eleven as the CURTAIN *rises. The set is empty*

There are a desk and swivel chair LC. *On the desk are three telephones—a red "hot line", a black external and a white internal intercom. Behind the desk is a bookcase;* L *of the desk there is a chair next to the window* DL; R *of the desk there is another chair and behind that, in the upstage wall* C, *there is a door which leads to the hall.* R *of the door are a drinks cabinet and a fireplace with a large club fender. A door* DR *leads to a retiring room; nearby is an armchair and* C *is a small round table and two chairs*

The door opens and Dick Marr (The Home Secretary) and Frances Cowdray (Leader of the House and Minister for the Arts) enter. They are both carrying briefcases and papers

Dick Why on earth do we have to have these late night meetings just before an election?

Frances I was meant to be going down to the constituency, now it will have to wait until the morning.

Dick And what did we achieve?

Frances Not a great deal—just Ray Turnbull muttering away as usual about being in the pocket of Washington and Randolph freezing him out of the discussion.

Dick (*eyeing the drinks cabinet*) I need a large whisky.

Frances I should wait if I were you. We don't want our "Prime Minister" getting offended. You know what a stickler he is for etiquette.

Dick I suppose we should be honoured by being asked to wait for a nightcap.

Frances Are you objecting to being part of what the press describe as "the Inner Circle"?

Dick (*shrugging*) No—not that I feel any great sense of security. Our leader doesn't believe in "collective cabinet decisions", he's a not very benevolent dictator.

Frances I shouldn't let him hear you say that. Are you worried about any cabinet reshuffle after the election?

Dick He's *indicated* I'll stay on at the Home Office but, well, you never know with him. How about you?

Frances I've had strong hints that I will get a better position.

Dick You deserve it of course, but I thought you liked your dual role as Leader of the House and Minister for the Arts.

Frances I do—but I want a more important ministry.

Dick Environment?

Frances Why not? I know Ray Turnbull is not keen on the idea—but I'm never sure just how much influence he has with Randolph.

Dick (*imitating Turnbull's slight accent*) He believes a woman's place is in the home, but he is deputy leader of course.

Frances Perhaps it would be wise to win the election before we start counting chickens.

Nigel, the Prime Minister's private secretary, enters

Nigel May I bring these in for the Prime Minister's signature?

Frances Of course, Nigel. Is he coming?

Nigel Any minute now. (*He crosses to the desk and lays out some papers*)

Ray Turnbull, the Foreign Secretary, enters, also with a briefcase which he is rifling through

Turnbull A most satisfactory meeting I thought.

Dick Did you?

Turnbull Randolph has such amazing energy—it's hard to keep up with him. (*To Nigel*) I seem to have mislaid that report on the Bonn meeting.

Nigel I'll have a copy sent round first thing in the morning, Minister.

Turnbull Thank you.

The Prime Minister, the Right Honourable Randolph Bolton, enters briskly

PM Have you got that letter ready, Nigel?

Nigel Yes, Prime Minister.

The Prime Minister sits at the desk and reads. Ignored, the others settle into chairs except Nigel who hovers deferentially. There is a long pause while Randolph Bolton studies the papers in front of him. Dick stifles a yawn. Frances gives him a warning glance. Ray Turnbull glances surreptitiously at his watch and starts to speak with some trepidation

Turnbull Er . . . Prime Minister——

The Prime Minister looks up irritably

PM (*sharply*) In a moment. (*He looks back at the papers*)

Turnbull Sorry . . .

The Prime Minister signs the paper and hands it to Nigel

PM Well that seems to be that. Is there any other business?

Dick No, Prime Minister, I'm sure you've covered *everything*.

Frances and Turnbull nod agreement

PM I'll leave you to draft the minutes, Nigel. Now I think we deserve a drink.

Frances An excellent executive decision.

PM (*with an imperious nod towards the drinks cabinet*) Dick.

Dick (*crossing to the drinks cabinet*) Certainly.

PM You were saying, Ray?

Turnbull As it is so late I wondered if you would mind me making a telephone call?

PM (*indicating the telephones*) Help yourself. I wouldn't advise the red one, unless you want to pass on the contents of our meeting to Washington.

There is a faint chuckle from Frances

Turnbull (*offended*) Sometimes I find it difficult to understand your humour, Randolph.

PM So I've noticed over the last twenty years.

Turnbull I won't disturb anyone, I'll make the call from the retiring room. (*He takes an address book from his briefcase*)

PM By all means.

Ray exits on his dignity

Dick (*taking a glass to Frances*) Brandy, Frances.

Frances Thank you.

Dick crosses with another glass to the PM who lights up a cigar

Dick (*almost hiding his distaste*) Your usual rum and tonic, Prime Minister. Shall I pour something for the Foreign Secretary?

Frances I'm sure he'll be leaving after his "private" call. Who can he be ringing at this time of night?

Dick Somehow I don't see Ray Turnbull having a mistress, so I presume it must be his wife.

Frances Then why did he need his address book?

PM Well, you've seen Enid. It's probably Freudian—he's trying to forget the number.

They all laugh sycophantically

Dick (*indicating the drinks*) Nigel?

Nigel No thank you. Do you need me any more, Prime Minister?

PM Oh! Sorry to have kept you up so late, dear boy.

Nigel Not at all. I'm only too pleased to help in any way.

PM (*avuncularly*) Well run along and get your beauty sleep. I expect to see you bright eyed and bushy tailed when I return from the constituency.

Nigel (*smiling*) I will be. Well er . . . goodnight. I know you don't need it, but May I wish you all good luck for the election?

PM Yes of course—we all need a little luck in politics. Thank you, Nigel, good-night.

They all call "good-night"

Nigel exits to the hall

What a conscientious young man.

Frances Indeed yes, and very loyal to you.

Dick (*casually*) He wears a very strong after shave.

Frances Is that what it is?

Dick I was beginning to think it was a hangover from when "that woman" used this room.

PM I had the place fumigated.

Dick Cleared the air in more ways than one.

PM Quite.

Dick (*changing the subject*) Talking of clearing the air—Ray is extremely touchy on the subject of the new American Laser one seven nine Deterrent Placement.

PM The less said about that the better. We'll finalize the matter after the election.

Frances There was so much fuss about the Missile bases over the years—we don't want another issue like that just before the country goes to the polls.

PM (*irritably*) Foreign governments are not going to finalize agreements just before an election.

Dick Quite—they might have to change them all next week.

The PM glares

Not that there's any risk in this case . . .

Frances The opinion polls are *most* encouraging.

Dick Let's hope there's no international crisis until it's been decided who's finger is on the trigger.

PM I can assure you it will be mine on the safety catch.

Turnbull enters

(*Pompously*) You can leave the Americans to me. I know how to handle them. There is no question of them being able to take any unilateral aggressive action with weapons sited on our soil.

Turnbull I'm glad to hear it. Personally I don't believe we should have even entertained the proposals in the first place.

Dick (*irritated*) For heaven's sake, Ray, we've been over this a dozen times. The decision has been taken . . .

PM (*firmly*) And the Foreign Secretary will abide by it. Won't you, Ray?

Turnbull (*reluctantly*) Yes of course—but that doesn't mean I agree with it.

Frances (*placating*) Don't worry, we can leave it to Randolph. He will act decisively once the election is over. Dual control will symbolize the renewed strength of Anglo-American relations.

PM Well put, Frances. (*Making a note*) I must remember that phrase. Dual control . . . renewed strength.

Turnbull (*packing his briefcase*) Thank you for the use of the phone, Randolph.

PM Satisfactory I hope.

Turnbull I had to ring Enid. It's the third time this week I've failed to get back for supper. I've been so busy.

Dick (*sarcastically*) You have a keen sense of duty, Ray.

Turnbull (*with a sour look*) An election is always a difficult time—but then of

course I've been involved in a few more than you, Dick. Well, I must be off.
Frances Good-night, Ray.
Dick Good-night.
PM Good luck with your television interview tomorrow.
Turnbull Thank you, Prime Minister.

Turnbull exits

PM I do hope he doesn't split too many infinitives. What is the latest on the opinion polls, Frances?
Frances (*beaming*) They are predicting a *nine* per cent lead. It's going to be a walkover.
Dick Thanks to Randolph. (*He toasts the PM*) It's all because of the "Bolton Charisma".
PM A dreadful media expression.
Frances But it's true—the country knows your worth.
PM (*with false modesty*) Well I hope I will have some influence on the result.
Dick Prime Minister, really, you don't have to fish for compliments. You know we all ride on your shoulders.
Frances Very broad shoulders. Speaking as Leader of the House I assure you the party is right behind you.
PM (*drily*) I often feel they'd like to be right behind me if I was standing on the edge of a cliff.
Frances Nonsense. We all hold you in great respect.
PM (*mellowing*) Well, it's nice to be appreciated sometimes. I must admit, if it was not for my ability to reconcile the vociferous extremes, the party would have disintegrated completely.
Dick There is a great spirit of party loyalty.
PM (*coldly*) I *am* the party.
Frances Quite ... Can I freshen your drink, Randolph?

The Prime Minister shakes his head

By the way, er ... have you given any further thought to a cabinet reshuffle?
PM (*abruptly*) Yes.
Dick (*hopefully*) Any conclusions?
PM That is an improper question at this time.
Dick (*ruffled*) I beg your pardon. I was only asking informally ... among friends.
PM There aren't any in politics. I suggest you concentrate your energies on making sure your constituents give you back your somewhat precarious seat.
Dick (*smiling, concealing his anger*) I don't have to worry, Randolph, they're not voting for me, they are voting for you. And you always know the right thing to say.
PM I believe I have a destiny and a duty to perform for the electorate. (*He rises in an involuntary political speech*) We must cast aside the outworn prejudices, discard the dogma of the extreme left or right. We must create a

new world with justice and freedom and . . . and . . . (*He clutches his heart*) Ahh! . . . Oh, God!

He staggers and leans against the mantelpiece. The others rise in concern

Dick What's the matter?
Frances (*anxiously*) Are you all right?
PM I don't know. I feel terrible.

He looks awful and his voice is weak. Frances guides him to a chair

Frances Let's get you to a chair, Randolph. Hold on to me. (*She helps him over to the armchair* DR)
Dick Can I do anything?
Frances Get some water. It may be just a very bad attack of indigestion.
Dick Right.

He goes to the drinks cabinet and returns with a glass of water. He gives it to Randolph who takes a drink

Frances How do you feel now?
PM I'll be all right. That's better. Now what was I saying?
Dick Justice and freedom — you were going through the party manifesto . . . again.
PM Yes. We must create an integrated society and break down the class and ethnic barriers. We . . . er . . . ethnic barriers . . . break down . . . aah . . . (*He staggers to his feet*)
Frances Randolph — is it worse?
PM It's like a clamp . . . steel fingers . . .
Dick Should I get a doctor?
PM Oh no . . . not now . . . not me . . . (*He clutches his chest and collapses*)
Dick Christ! Is he . . . he's not . . .?
Frances I think so. (*She moves to the body and kneels down*)
Dick I'll get an ambulance.
Frances No, there isn't time, out of my way. (*She starts to give him the kiss of life and massages his heart. She stops*)
Dick Good God! Can't you continue to give him the kiss of life? It's not as if it's the first time.
Frances I'm afraid there's no life left to kiss. He's gone.
Dick I can't believe it.
Frances Don't just stand there, do something useful.
Dick We must get an ambulance. (*He crosses to the desk and picks up the telephone receiver*)
Frances Put it down!
Dick What?
Frances Get me some brandy instead. Do you want to be Home Secretary in the next government? Then *put it down*. He's dead. The country goes to the polls in about thirty hours. Without him we could lose.

Dick replaces the telephone receiver

Dick (*nodding agreement*) We almost certainly will. (*Hopelessly*) Oh! God . . . what are we going to do?

Frances (*icily calm*) We are going to think very carefully before we do anything.

Dick (*flustered*) But what about Randolph?

Frances I don't think he cares any more. (*She pours herself a drink*)

Pause

Dick Shouldn't we inform somebody? The Queen? The Minister of Health?

Frances (*thinking*) Probably. But five minutes won't make much difference.

Dick Are you sure he's dead? Should we call the police?

Frances Do you suspect foul play?

Dick Certainly not.

Frances Well you are Home Secretary, therefore the police—so to speak, already know. It's a heart attack.

Pause

Dick Yes, of course . . . (*Drinking deeply—a terrible thought!!*) Turnbull!

Frances What?

Dick He's Deputy Prime Minister. He's bound to take over as . . . oh, God!

Frances So don't telephone. Don't move until we've had time to *think*!

Dick (*horrified*) Turnbull . . . after all we've been through . . . not Turnbull! (*He paces across the room*)

Frances (*acidly*) Yes, Ray Turnbull . . . as Leader of the Opposition— without Randolph I believe we'll lose (*anticipating*) even with the opinion polls' nine per cent prediction. Randolph *is* the party.

Dick Was.

Frances Quite. (*After a pause*) Why not still is?

Dick (*blankly*) What?

Frances If everyone assumed Randolph was alive we'd win the election— right?

Dick Agreed.

Frances So we must keep him alive for another couple of days.

Dick Are we going into the resurrection business?

Frances I'm serious.

Dick (*realizing*) You are, aren't you?

Frances Deadly serious.

Dick (*grimly*) A most appropriate adverb.

Frances (*pacing*) Perhaps you should apply that expensively educated mind of yours to the problem in hand.

Dick (*distastefully looking at the corpse*) I can't think straight with him lying there. Never could stand the pompous ass anyway.

Frances (*decisively*) We must move him into the retiring room quickly in case anyone comes in. (*She opens the retiring room door*)

Dick (*hesitating*) Look—are you sure about this? I mean my car is waiting to take me to my constituency. I ought to be with them at this time. The party workers have been so loyal, so . . .

Frances So you owe it to them. Come on. You take his arms.

She picks up his legs. Reluctantly Dick does as he's told and together they drag his body into the retiring room

The intercom phone buzzes

Frances appears at the door. The buzzer goes again. She takes a deep breath and answers

Yes? ... I see. Thank you. (*She replaces the receiver*) Dick. Dick!

Dick appears, breathing heavily

Dick He's on the bed. Who was that?
Frances Turnbull, he's on his way up.
Dick Oh, God!
Frances Sit down. Be normal.
Dick Normal!?
Frances Relax. Have a drink.
Dick I need one.

She pushes him into a chair and a drink into his hand and sits herself as there is a knock on the hall door

Frances Come in.

Ray Turnbull enters from the hall

Turnbull Sorry to interrupt, PM but ... oh ...?
Frances (*whispering and pointing to the retiring room door*) He's having a nap.
Turnbull (*disbelieving*) Nap? Ah ... of course. He must be exhausted. (*Sycophantically as if Randolph could hear*) Such an amazing man, such charisma. (*He moves* DR)
Dick I used the word myself a few minutes ago ... before he ... left us.
Turnbull Such political instinct—but with such heart, such integrity. A tireless worker for our party.
Frances He's a bit weary now.
Turnbull I left my address book by the telephone, I'm afraid.
Dick (*quickly*) I'll get it for you.
Turnbull No—don't bother—I'll be careful not to wake him.

Before they can stop him he exits to the retiring room

Dick and Frances look at each other in horror

Turnbull re-enters carrying an address book and very carefully shuts the door. He turns and looks at them

He looks tired out. (*Shaking his head as he goes to the hall door*) I dread to think what would happen to *us* all if anything happened to *him*. Good-night!

He exits to the hall

Frances Good-night again.
Dick (*weakly*) 'Night, Ray. So what do we do now? Say he's sick and hope

no-one finds out till after they've counted the votes?

Frances Possible . . . but I can see so many snags.

Dick His wife to start with . . .

Frances And his Cabinet colleagues would call — and we would have to bring in a doctor . . .

Dick (*irritably*) So what do *you* suggest?

Frances (*concentrating*) There must be a way — it's only for two or three days.

Dick What we need is a double, like that chap on television.

Frances No, the last thing we need is a comic impressionist. But you've given me an idea. We want someone who looks exactly like Randolph. (*Excitedly*) Jackson!

Dick Jackson?

Frances Yes, Jackson. James. Johnny. *Gerry!* Gerry Jackson. (*She stands and moves* C)

Dick What are you talking about?

Frances Don't you remember? I told you about him a couple of years ago.

Dick Did you?

Frances Of course I did. Don't you remember?

Dick (*shrugging*) Yes, vaguely.

Frances Gerry Jackson is an actor.

Dick Never heard of him.

Frances Hardly anyone has. In my capacity as Minister for the Arts I once visited a small repertory theatre in Lincolnshire a couple of years ago; and I saw a play, Strindberg or Coward, something like that.

Dick I sometimes wonder how you've kept the job.

Frances There was an actor playing a small part who stood out. I can remember him vividly.

Dick Was he so good?

Frances I don't recall — but he bore such a striking resemblance to Randolph, even his voice. I was quite distracted from the play. I've often thought we could use him in a documentary or something.

Dick You're not suggesting . . .?

Frances Why not? It's only for a short time. (*She crosses to the bookcase and takes out a telephone book*)

Dick (*appalled*) Have you totally taken leave of your senses? An actor as leader of the country? That's ridiculous!

Frances (*looking through the telephone book for the number*) He'll just be a temporary stand-in. It's only going to be for seventy-two hours. (*Getting enthusiastic*) Randolph has already recorded his television speech — that's being broadcast tomorrow, so that's one hurdle out of the way.

Dick What about his constituency? His political agent is bound to see through it.

Frances Hmm. I don't think so. Not if we're careful. When you see him you'll understand.

Dick (*disbelieving*) I can't wait.

Frances (*looking at the directory*) Jackson. Gerald. Got it. I must think of a good excuse to get him over. (*She dials on the external phone*)

Dick It had better be—it's past midnight. Now don't say anything specific. Don't make commitments. Don't ...

Frances Shh! It's ringing.

Dick (*after a pause*) He's probably not at home.

Frances (*into the phone*) Mr Jackson? ... Ah! Good ... I'm sorry to telephone at this hour but it is urgent ... Of course, silly of me—I'm Frances Cowdray, Minister for the Arts and ... (*to Dick*) He's hung up.

Dick I'm not surprised. It's a ridiculous idea anyway.

Frances (*dialling*) Don't close your mind till you see him. (*Into the phone*) Mr Jackson, *please* don't hang up! I really am Frances Cowdray ... I am telephoning from Number Ten ... (*Raising her eyes to heaven*) *Downing Street*. It is just possible that we have an important part to offer you ... Yes, a film ... About the election ... That's why it is urgent ... We have to shoot tomorrow ... There would be a fee of course ... Yes, a *substantial* fee ... Well could you come over now? ... Yes, I know it's very late ... I believe this could be of national importance ... Perhaps your agent could wait until after the interview? ... Good. Thank you. I'll tell Security to expect you ... Number Ten. (*She replaces the receiver*)

Dick He's coming round?

Frances Yes. He'll be here soon, he only lives in Pimlico. (*She picks up the intercom phone*) I'm speaking for the Prime Minister. He's expecting a Mr Jackson. Show him up please. (*She replaces the receiver*) Now how are we going to convince him? (*She sits in the desk chair*)

Dick And even if we do—what about the body? We can't leave it in there. Oh! This is ridiculous. We'll end up in jail, our careers ruined ...

Frances The alternative is worse.

Dick We'll be playing Russian roulette with a machine gun.

Frances And if we don't do anything our careers are ruined anyway. We'll be in the wilderness for years—with Ray Turnbull as our leader.

Dick (*this really hurts*) Turnbull! Oh, all right let's see this Jackson. I don't suppose he'll do it anyway. (*He sits by the desk*)

Frances He'll have to be paid of course. You can afford it, you're wealthy.

Dick Not since we put up the income tax. (*He has pulled himself together*) Frances, I think I see a way of coping with this problem of the body. I'll speak to Colonel Hardacre.

Frances looks

He's in charge of Security here at Number Ten. He reports to Scotland Yard, of course—but I suspect he's also M.I.5.

Frances You're the Home Secretary, don't you *know*?

Dick They tell me as little as possible and I prefer it that way.

Frances I see. Well, if we make our story outrageous enough he'll probably believe it.

Dick It shouldn't be too difficult to convince him this is a Russian plot.

Frances Just assume for a moment that Jackson could get away with it. How long do you think we should try and keep it up?

Dick Till after the election and for as long as it takes to lobby the people that matter and make sure Turnbull does not get the job. But how do we arrange Randolph's death?

Frances Hmm . . . He could have a nervous breakdown on a trip abroad. His clothes could be found on the . . . no.

Dick No, not that again. It will be best to keep it simple. If we can arrange for the body to be deep frozen, then we can, at the appropriate moment, thaw it out and announce that Randolph died of a heart attack.

Frances (*nodding approval*) We'll work out the details later, but first we must deal with the priorities. (*She is vibrant and decisive*)

Dick Do you have any idea what Jackson's politics are?

Frances No.

Dick It could be important if he happens to feel strongly.

Frances If we decide the idea is feasible we'll sound him out.

Dick Feasible! I think you've been reading too many paperbacks.

Frances (*not put down at all*) It's so preposterous it could work! How often do you really look closely at people you know well?

Dick What do you mean?

Frances If your secretary or your uncle or the doorman at your club are in the right place at the right time, it wouldn't occur to you to doubt their authenticity would it?

Dick Well . . .

Frances Unless they had drastically changed their appearance in some way.

Dick (*thoughtfully*) That's true I suppose.

Frances Well the Prime Minister will be in the right place at the right time, and coached by us he'll say the right things.

Dick (*with some enthusiasm*) I suppose it's just possible . . . but he's not my secretary, he's the Prime Minister.

Frances All the more reason for him to be accepted. Very few people risk the disapproval of a senior or powerful person by doubting them in any way, or rudely peering into their face. Now, what about Eva?

Dick (*anxiously*) She was here earlier. Didn't she go to the opera?

Frances Yes. (*She lifts the intercom and buzzes*) Mrs Cowdray here again. Could you tell me, has Mrs Bolton returned? . . . I see. No thank you, the Prime Minister wanted to know, that's all. (*She replaces the phone. To Dick*) She came back half an hour ago and was told Randolph was in conference so she went straight up to the bedroom suite.

Dick If she comes down it's all over. (*He stands, agitated*) It's not too late — (*his voice rises*) — Frances, we haven't done anything unretractable yet.

Frances Dick! Calm down. You are Home Secretary, remember. You are supposed to keep a cool head in a crisis.

Dick Somebody else's crisis. I feel as if my head could end up in a basket.

Frances Calm!

Dick Right! (*He pours himself a drink*) Just to settle the nerves.

Frances Well, go easy, you'll need to think clearly. (*She sits at the desk and begins making notes*)

Dick What are you doing?

Frances Making a list of the pitfalls — so we can avoid them. Have we a copy of the Official Secrets Act for signature?

Dick Good Lord—*I* don't know. Why do you want one?
Frances There will come a moment when we have to tell Jackson *something*. He could prove unreliable.

Dick opens a couple of drawers and finds a copy of the Official Secrets Act which he lay on the desk

Dick (*panicking*) If he rushes out and tells the newspapers . . . we'll be ruined for nothing . . .
Frances And who is going to believe an out-of-work actor as opposed to two Ministers of the Crown? (*She stands*)
Dick (*seeing the logic*) I see what you mean.
Frances (*making a decision*) Call Colonel Hardacre, Dick. (*She crosses front stage*)
Dick What now?
Frances Make the appointment in an hour or so — by that time we'll have to tell someone something.
Dick (*picking up the phone and hesitating*) You do it.
Frances Don't be pathetic. You're the Home Secretary.
Dick (*dialling*) The PM is head of the Service you know, I'm consulted of course but——
Frances (*irritably*) Well as Minister for the Arts I'm not even consulted, except about a pile of bricks at the Tate Gallery.

She exits into the retiring room

Dick Hardacre? . . . Marr here. . . . *Richard* Marr . . . Home Secretary. . . . Yes, very late. . . . The Prime Minister wants to see you. . . . No, tonight, it's urgent. By all means get dressed first. . . . In about an hour. Thank you.

Frances appears at the door holding a wallet and keys

(*Replacing the receiver*) I wonder how he'd react if I'd said World War Three had broken out?
Frances If we don't get our story right it probably will. (*She puts the wallet and keys in her briefcase*)
Dick But we'll have more than four minutes to worry about it.
Frances More like four years I should imagine. Dick?
Dick Yes?
Frances We'll have to hide the body in case anyone else wants to use the bathroom.
Dick Good heavens! Where?
Frances Under the bed.
Dick That's where the Reds usually are!

She exits into the retiring room followed by a reluctant Dick

The buzzer goes

After a moment, Frances appears as the buzzer goes again

Frances (*calling into the retiring room*) Tidy things up and hurry. (*She* *answers the phone)* Yes? . . . Thank you. Send him up . . . (*She replaces the receiver*)

Dick enters, looking flustered

Dick He's heavier than I thought. It seems rather undignified shoving the Prime Minister of Great Britain under the bed.
Frances The late Prime Minister.

There is a knock on the door

And here is the understudy, I hope.
Dick (*muttering*) Not knowing a line of the part.

Dick sits in the chair by the window. Frances sits behind the PM's desk

Frances (*calling*) Come in.

Nervously, Gerry Jackson enters from the hall. He looks as unlike the PM as possible, wearing a moustache, rather scruffy casual clothes and a different hairstyle

Good-evening, Mr Jackson. (*She rises and holds out her hand with a charming smile*)
Gerry Hello.
Frances I'm Frances Cowdray and this is the Home Secretary, Mr Marr.

Dick stands and crosses to Gerry

Gerry Er . . . hello. (*He shakes hands warily*)
Dick Do sit down, Mr Jackson. So good of you to come at this unearthly hour.

Gerry sits where indicated. There is a pause while Frances sits. Dick, who moves behind Gerry, shakes his head and indicates to Frances that as far as he is concerned the whole thing is off

Frances Mr Jackson, you must be wondering what is so vital that cannot wait until morning.
Gerry I am more than a little curious.
Frances Have you ever been told that you bear a resemblance to the Prime Minister?
Gerry Frequently. A few years ago it happened all the time. That's why I grew this moustache. It used to drive me mad.
Dick Why was that?
Gerry It rather limited my choice of parts.
Dick Quite.
Frances Well right now that attribute could be of vital importance. In fact I can say of national importance.
Gerry Really?
Frances For reasons of security I cannot go into the details at the moment.
Gerry Do I gather you want me to play the part of the Prime Minister in some documentary film or something? Presumably to be shot over the election period?

Frances How very discerning of you. It has a lot to do with the election and that is why we have to make a very quick decision as it will mean starting immediately.

Dick Quite frankly—although I can see a likeness of course, I do not believe Mr Jackson could pass close scrutiny, I think it would be best if we reconsidered the situation, Frances, (*to Gerry*) and of course, I apologize for any inconvenience we have caused you and we would be happy to recompense you for any expense incurred.

Frances I wonder if you would be prepared to co-operate to some extent, Mr Jackson?

Gerry Certainly. Would you like me to audition?

Dick That won't be necessary.

Gerry If you have a copy of the script I will read for you. I'm not particularly good at sight reading, I prefer to have time to study the part thoroughly but——

Frances (*trying to interrupt*) Mr Jackson, I——

Gerry —it would give you an idea of my suitability. In this instance I do know something of the character, of course. That is the public persona, but then I do not suppose you will be filming the domestic and personal side——

Dick (*firmly*) Mr Jackson!

Gerry Yes?

Frances We won't require you to read. I have seen you perform and have no doubts about your professional ability. But I would like you to help us come to a decision by putting Mr Marr's mind at rest about your appearance.

Gerry In what way?

Frances Would you be prepared to shave off your moustache—and perhaps slip into some other clothes?

Gerry (*surprised*) I'm not sure I want the part yet ... and it would take me three weeks to grow this again.

Dick You probably have other engagements coming up?

Gerry Oh, yes. There's a TV serial that I'm up for and I'm considering a tour and——

Frances But nothing is actually signed?

Gerry Well ... er ... not exactly signed.

Frances Perhaps we could pay you a special fee even if you don't get offered the role.

Gerry I should speak to my agent ...

Dick I doubt whether he would welcome a discussion at this hour.

Gerry Hm ... yes. You have a point. As a matter of fact my agent does not welcome discussions at any hour.

Dick What sum do you think would be acceptable?

Gerry (*trying to strengthen his hand*) You know I once did a sketch—playing the part of Randolph Bolton—everyone was amazed.

Dick (*shortly*) Really.

Gerry Yes. I watched him very closely on TV and got some of his mannerisms. You know——

Frances (*interrupting*) In view of the urgency, perhaps you would consider audition expenses of say, one hundred pounds.

Gerry (*smiling*) Oh! What the hell! For a hundred pounds I'd probably shave off a beard. Have you a bathroom? (*He stands*)

Frances Of course. Dick, take Mr Jackson next door and ... er ... you'll find some suitable clothes in the wardrobe.

Dick I feel we are wasting time——

Frances glares at him

— but of course why not try? This way, Mr Jackson.

He leads the way out and Jackson follows, through to the retiring room

Gerry (*as he exits*) If we're working together, Minister, you must call me Gerry.

They exit

Frances, still seated in the Prime Minister's chair, jumps as the phone rings — the red phone

Frances Hello. ... No, this is Mrs Cowdray the Leader of the House. ... Who? ... I'm sorry, please tell the President the Prime Minister is ... er ... indisposed at the moment. Can I give him a message? ... Yes, certainly I will tell him. He's feeling very confident about the outcome. ... Please give his thanks to the President. Goodbye. (*She replaces the phone*)

Dick enters

Dick Frances, this is ridiculous. How on earth can you expect it to work? He doesn't look anything like Randolph. He might fool people at a distance, but close-up, well, forget it. I mean his colleagues, his private secretary and his *wife*. Eva would know instantly.

Frances Eva and Randolph see as little of each other as possible — but you are probably right. It was a foolish notion. I remember him differently.

Gerry (*off*) Where do I find the clothes?

Dick Just coming.

He shrugs and exits to the retiring room

Frances picks up the phone and presses the intercom button

Frances Hello. ... Yes, this is Mrs Cowdray again. The Prime Minister does not wish to be interrupted by anyone or by any calls ... except Colonel Hardacre. ... Ring me before you show him up, please. Thank you.

There is a knock on the hall door

Damn, yes ...

Eva enters

Ah — good-evening, Eva. I thought you'd gone to bed.

Eva Not yet. I've been to the opera, it makes me sleepy, but not tired. I thought you were in conference with Randolph.

Frances I'm just waiting to take an important call for him. He's having a nap.
(*She indicates the retiring room*)

Dick enters and stops guiltily as he sees Eva

Eva Hello, Dick. Were you having a nap too?
Dick I ... er ... good-evening, Eva. I didn't know you were here.
Frances Is he asleep, Dick?
Dick Yes. Worn out, exhausted. I was ... er ... just using the bathroom.

Frances stands and moves to the window

Frances (*talking nervously*) The President rang and Colonel Hardacre is
coming over, and ... and ... Turnbull has——
Eva (*interrupting*) Well, I'm going to bed. If Randolph is going to be up for
hours would you suggest he sleeps down here in the retiring room? I don't
want to be woken up at four in the morning again.
Dick Yes, of course.
Eva Not that we share the same bedroom, but he has the most irritating habit
of opening my door to ask if I am asleep. He then stamps around and
gargles at the top of his lungs.
Dick Oh, dear.
Eva (*without enthusiasm*) And Frances, can you let him know my bags are
packed ready for our visit to the constituency tomorrow. And I've
rehearsed my dutiful wife speech. (*She moves downstage to face Frances*)
Frances (*laughing nervously*) Randolph can always rely on you, Eva.
Eva Yes, he can—but can I always rely on Randolph?

*The retiring room door opens and carrying a shoe, Gerry enters, looking
exactly like Randolph. He stops as he sees Eva*

Gerry I'm having trouble with the shoe ... Oh! (*His reaction is rapid—an
actor ad-libbing*) Good-evening, my dear. (*He smiles brightly at her*)
Eva Dick was just saying you were exhausted. You look pretty bright to me.
Gerry I ... er ... am tired (*suddenly weary*) but there's so much to do at the
moment.
Eva (*insincerely*) Well, don't *over*do it. The nation needs you, Randolph.
Frances Eva's right—you must conserve your energies, Prime Minister.
Gerry (*pompously*) Someone has to steer the ship of state.
Eva (*sarcastically*) We can all sleep well knowing you are at the helm.
Talking of bed, try not to wake me up. I suggest you stay down here,
Randolph. Goodnight. (*She moves nearer to him and looks at the shoe*)
Gerry Yes, of course. Good-night.
Eva (*indicating the shoe—sweetly*) Try putting your foot in it as usual.

Eva exits to the hall

There is a stunned silence

Gerry (*smiling confidently*) Do I get the part?
Dick (*amazed*) She didn't bat an eyelid!
Frances (*sinking into a chair, relieved*) What did I tell you, Dick?

Dick (*open-mouthed*) He's a dead ringer. He could be the clone.

Gerry sits R of the round table

Gerry Now perhaps we can get down to the details.

Dick (*pouring a drink*) Yes, of course. Would you like a drink?

Gerry A small Scotch, please.

Dick I wonder if you could get used to rum and tonic?

Gerry I very much doubt it. Why?

Frances I am afraid that's what the PM prefers.

Gerry Odd chap. Still that will hardly be noticed on film.

Dick (*bringing him a whisky*) Your whisky. Right, before we go any further, can we have your complete assurance that everything you are about to hear is in the strictest confidence? (*He sits L of the round table*)

Gerry (*taking the drink*) I suppose so.

Frances I am afraid we must insist. In fact you will have to sign the Official Secrets Act. (*She lays a paper and pen on the table in front of him*)

Gerry (*looking at the paper*) I never sign anything until I've checked the small print. You have to be very careful nowadays to see that the cable and video rights have been covered. Then there is the question of the billing and——

Frances No billing!

Dick What? I thought this was the leading part?

Dick It is the most important part you will ever play. (*Seriously*) Do you think you could impersonate the Prime Minister for a few days—so convincingly that no-one would guess you were not him?

Gerry You mean . . . not on film?

Frances Exactly.

Gerry Live? I don't know . . . I suppose it depends on the script.

Dick No script.

Gerry Ad lib? . . . Well I should expect a percentage of the author's royalties——

Frances Would one hundred thousand pounds interest you?

Dick does a double-take. Gerry sits up and thinks hard

Gerry (*looking at her disbelievingly*) It would certainly help to concentrate my mind.

Frances Mr Marr would pay you fifty thousand pounds tomorrow and a further fifty thousand if you succeed in the deception . . . er . . . role.

Dick goes white

Gerry (*musing*) No script and no billing and no director . . .

Francis And absolute secrecy. This really is of international importance. (*She pauses*)

Gerry (*smiling*) It's certainly a challenge . . . (*making up his mind*) and it beats three episodes of *Crossroads*—Right, you've got a deal. Where do I sign?

Frances Here. (*She indicates*)

Gerry signs in the somewhat contorted way used by left-handers

Thank you, Prime Minister. (*She folds the paper thoughtfully and puts it in her bag*)

Dick is pouring another drink with a shaking hand

I think I'll join you in a small brandy, Home Secretary . . . and a rum and tonic for Randolph.

Gerry (*shrugging*) Well if it helps to get into the part. No, I'm sorry my stomach can't take rum. I'll have another small Scotch, please. (*He stands and moves to the drinks cabinet*)

Frances If this is going to succeed the smallest detail is vital.

Gerry Of course.

Frances (*steely*) So you'd better remember that Randolph was *right*-handed.

Dick turns sharply

Dick You mean he's *not*?

Frances He just signed with his left.

Gerry (*easily*) Don't worry, among my many talents I am almost ambidextrous. I won't forget.

Dick You'd better not.

Gerry I'll remember in future. If I'd known I'd been voting for a chap who drinks rum and tonic . . .

Dick Well, I'm glad to hear you did vote for him. (*Handing out drinks*) Here's to the party and to us.

Gerry takes the glass with his left hand and ostentatiously changes it to his right. They raise their glasses and drink. During the following dialogue Gerry sits behind the desk

Gerry If you don't mind, I'll just check my props. I suppose you will eventually tell me why I have to impersonate the Prime Minister?

Frances (*quietly*) Just over an hour ago Randolph Bolton dropped dead of a heart attack.

Gerry chokes quietly on his drink

It will be your job to convince *everyone* he's still alive . . . at least till after the election. Can you do it, you'll be fully briefed by us?

Gerry Good God! Where is the . . . er . . . body? (*He takes another swig*)

Dick In there under the bed . . .

Gerry reacts again

Gerry But w—w—what are we, you, going to do about that?

Frances M.I.5. Mr Marr is Home Secretary, after all. The matter will be dealt with by Colonel Hardacre.

The buzzer goes and Gerry absently answers. Dick and Frances freeze

Gerry (*into the phone*) Yes. . . . Colonel Hardacre? (*He realizes what he is doing*) Thank you. (*He replaces the receiver*) He's on his way up. (*He sinks back into the chair*)

Frances You deal with him, Dick, I'll continue with the briefing.

Dick But what exactly am I supposed to say——

Frances (*interrupting*) As little as possible—Remember it's a plot—some foreign power tried to assassinate the Prime Minister.

Gerry What am *I* supposed to say?
Frances As——

There is a knock on the door to the hall

Gerry Come in.

Colonel Hardacre opens the door and enters

Colonel Good-evening, Prime Minister. Or rather good-morning. You sent for me I believe? (*Stuffily*) A matter of national security . . . at one a.m. . . . .
Gerry Yes, Colonel (*with an edge*) I'm afraid the interests of the country have to come before your beauty sleep.
Colonel (*put out*) I'm sorry, sir. I did not mean to infer——
Gerry (*firmly*) I'm sure you didn't. The Home Secretary will put you in the picture and I trust you will deal with the matter with expediency and discretion.
Colonel Sir!
Gerry This evening, there has been an attempt on my life.
Colonel What??
Dick Would you come this way please, Colonel?
Colonel (*with alacrity*) Yes, sir.

He follows Dick into the retiring room

Frances Well done! I think we have a chance. (*She sits by the desk and takes out her piece of paper and makes notes*) The main problem areas are personal. Your wife Eva to start with.
Gerry Oh yes, what am I going to do about her? Are we close?
Frances Fortunately not—but she is going to travel up with you to the constituency tomorrow. (*Thinking*) We'll arrange a last minute change of plan so you can go separately.
Gerry Good.

During this time Frances quietly moves to the retiring room door and tests it is shut and then sits L of the round table

Frances Your election agent's name is Saunders. As I remember he's got red sideburns so you can't miss him. You call him Jack. Then there is the acceptance speech. (*She is writing with nervous excitement*)
Gerry You mean the one that goes: "Mr Returning Officer. I would like to thank you and your staff for the efficient and courteous way——"
Frances That's the one.
Gerry (*continuing, carried away*) "—and all you wonderful helpers who have striven to bring the message of our great party to the voters. And I promise to represent not only *my* voters but *all* my constituents, and further more——"
Frances (*drily*) I should keep it brief, if I were you.
Gerry I was beginning to enjoy it. By the way I am not a political animal. I even avoid Equity meetings. I can't stand all that shouting.
Frances Politics is not a gentleman's game—which is probably why I am doing so well at it.

Gerry I hope this place is not bugged. Do you really think we can pull this off?

Frances Yes. (*She stands and moves to the desk*) God you look exactly like him—makes me feel strange. (*She sits in the chair* R *of the desk*)

Gerry Why exactly?

Frances (*sharply*) Back to business.

Gerry (*shrugging*) I must tell you I am not a regular member of your party, and to be perfectly honest I am not quite sure what you stand for.

Frances Very few people are but as this is only a short engagement I should not bother to try and swot it up. We'll concentrate on the more immediate problems of survival. Fortunately Randolph has very few intimate friends—the more you got to know him the less you liked him.

Gerry And that applies to Eva?

Frances Yes. They've been . . . er . . . distant for years. Randolph—was never very discreet about his affairs.

Gerry (*looking up sharply*) I see. I wonder why she stayed with him. She seems such an attractive woman.

Frances He could be a very attractive man when he wanted to be. (*Sharply*) I really do not think this is necessary.

Gerry If you say so, but the more background knowledge I have the better . . . and it was you who brought the matter up.

Frances Yes, I'm sorry.

Gerry (*understanding*) Oh not at all. The wound is obviously deep.

Frances It was years ago. (*Bitterly*) He ruined my marriage and used me.

Gerry And yet you have continued to work with him?

Frances If you only worked with people you respected you would find it very limiting in politics. (*She stands and moves round the desk to stand behind him*)

Gerry Like an actor—your first duty is survival.

Frances Exactly. (*She hears a noise at the door*) Careful.

Hardacre and Dick enter from the retiring room

Gerry Yes, Hardacre—what is your opinion?

Colonel You have been extremely lucky, sir. They must have used plastic surgery to get such an incredible likeness.—I can see why he fooled the Security Guards.

Gerry Not a very efficient system.

Colonel No, sir. Heads will roll I assure you.

Frances Unfortunately that is impossible, Colonel. Nobody—I repeat *nobody* must know of this yet. Isn't that so, Prime Minister?

Gerry Absolutely.

Colonel If you say so, sir. I gather you surprised him in here and he had a heart attack.

Gerry Nearly gave me one too.

Dick Colonel, you'll arrange to keep the body on ice until you get further instructions.

Colonel Yes, sir. You can leave it all to me. Two of my men will be over in a few minutes. (*He starts to leave*) Of course it wouldn't have happened if I had been here myself. I would have known he was not you, sir.

Gerry I am sure you would.

Colonel Oh! Yes. On close inspection there was a marked difference. He had a distinctly shifty look about him.

Gerry Really. Well ... er ... I didn't have time to study him in detail. It was quite an unnerving experience, seeing myself standing there.

Colonel What exactly happened, Prime Minister? (*He moves to the desk*)

Gerry Well ... (*gathering his thoughts and improvizing*) ... we came back earlier than expected ...

Frances (*quickly*) From a working dinner.

Colonel He had obviously misjudged the time.

Gerry Obviously. He was ... er ...

Dick (*quickly*) Going through the drawers of the desk, I think you said, Prime Minister.

Gerry Yes. Then he saw me. He seemed absolutely amazed ...

Colonel Did either of you speak?

Gerry There wasn't time. He clutched at his chest, groaned ... and ... collapsed, on the floor just over there.

Frances We were just behind. I rushed over to him and realized he was dead.

Colonel How could you be so sure?

Frances I was once a nurse. It was a heart attack.

Colonel I see. Then you telephoned me.

Dick That is correct.

Colonel Why did you tell me not to come at once?

Gerry ⎫ (*together*) ⎧ We were considering ...
Frances ⎭   ⎩ The Prime Minister needed time to assess the situation.

Dick I am sure you must appreciate that this incident could have international repercussions if it is not handled with great delicacy.

Colonel Of course, Minister. It could have been very dangerous. Imagine having a Russian spy as Prime Minister.

Frances You're sure he was Russian?

Colonel Yes. It's amazing how they slip up on little details. Everything perfect except the tie. It was purchased at Gum in Moscow.

Gerry (*amazed*) Really? Extraordinary.

Dick You will not even discuss this with your superior, Colonel.

Colonel (*protesting*) But, Home Secretary, I really must insist ...

Gerry (*trying his best*) No, you will report directly to Mr Marr ... or myself of course.

Colonel (*reluctantly*) Yes, sir. If you say so.

Gerry I do. Thank you. That will be all for now. Good-night.

Colonel Good-night, sir.

Colonel Hardacre exits to the hall

Frances So far, so good. What was that about the tie?

Dick He was given it on his last trip to Moscow.

Gerry Bloody lucky! Now to business.

Frances Yes. Let's continue with the briefing.

Gerry I was thinking about the money.

Dick Ah! Yes . . . er . . . would you mind collecting it in Switzerland? I . . . er
. . . have some funds there you see and . . . er . . .

Frances (*amused*) I am sure the Chancellor would be most interested.

Dick (*angrily*) Well I can hardly pop round the corner to Nat West, and draw
it out in used fivers without causing some speculation, can I?

Frances (*placatingly*) No, of course not. I am sure Mr Jackson—
Randolph—understands.

Gerry Perfectly—but I need *something* up front—*in cash*. (*Quickly*) Not that
I don't trust you, of course—but when you've been a touring actor for
years you learn to be careful.

Dick Would ten per cent of the first payment be acceptable tomorrow?

Gerry Ten per cent? Where have I heard those magic words before? (*Steely*)
Ten per cent of the *overall* figure would ensure even greater enthusiasm
from me.

Frances Right, that's agreed. Dick, you'll bring the money here in the
morning.

Dick Oh! All right. Let's get one thing straight. (*He glares at Gerry through
frightened and vicious eyes*) This is not a game, Jackson. If anything goes
wrong you'll be the first to suffer.

Gerry I am aware of that. I quite understand.

Dick (*hard*) I hope so. (*Looking at his watch*) I have to go now. You'll sleep
down here, Jackson. That should keep you out of harm's way until
morning.

Gerry Right. Do you know the names of the staff?

Frances Don't worry, I'll fill you in with as much as I can, and I will return by
breakfast time. It is not unusual for us to have breakfast meetings
nowadays. An unfortunate American habit.

Gerry I don't usually rise till noon.

There is a noise off in the retiring room

Frances (*jumping*) What's that?

*They freeze. They all wait anxiously. Frances indicates that Dick should
investigate. He moves quietly to the door and throws it open*

Hardacre stands there

Colonel Just moving the body, sir. No need to be concerned.

Dick Yes—of course. Thank you. (*He closes the door*)

Frances That was careless. We didn't lock the outer door.

Dick (*collecting his briefcase*) I'll be back at ten a.m. Good-night. And don't
let me down, Jackson, you'll be sorry if you do.

Dick exits to the hall

*Gerry looks at Frances with an amused smile on his face. Frances meets his gaze
coolly*

Gerry (*seriously*) He meant that, didn't he?

Frances (*nodding*) I wouldn't like him for an enemy. He has power and
money and great ambition.

Gerry A dangerous combination.

Frances looks at Gerry thoughtfully as she takes out the bunch of keys and the wallet and hands them to Gerry

Frances Yes. Don't make the mistake of underestimating Dick Marr. Now here are Randolph's things. You'll have to work out which key goes where. I know he has a private file and a drawer he always keeps locked.

Gerry The keys of the Kingdom. I hope this works ... and if it doesn't, perhaps you'll come over from Holloway and we'll perform *Private Lives* together at the Scrubs.

CURTAIN

SCENE 2

The same. Three days later. Late afternoon

As the CURTAIN *rises Eva enters from the hall carrying a vase of flowers. She puts them down on the round table and starts to arrange them*

Nigel enters

Nigel Isn't Randolph ready yet?

Eva No, not quite. Have you got problems, Nigel?

Nigel No—it's just that the Foreign Secretary has an appointment and he's getting rather impatient.

Eva Oh all right, send him up, I'll cope.

Nigel Thank you so much. I usually do the flowers.

Nigel exits and returns a few moments later followed by Ray Turnbull

The Foreign Secretary, Mrs Bolton.

Eva Thank you, Nigel.

Nigel exits to the hall

Good-afternoon, Ray. Congratulations.

They shake hands

Turnbull Good-afternoon, Eva. Congratulations all round are in order, I believe. How is our leader today? He must be feeling gratified by the splendid vote of confidence that the country has given him.

Eva Yes, he's in remarkably good form. He seems to have taken on a new lease of life ... as well as on this place. (*She turns and continues arranging flowers*)

Turnbull I hope he's remembered that we arranged to meet.

Eva I'm sure he has. He's just changing after his audience with the Queen.

Turnbull Ah! That's what I am here about. I expect he'll want to discuss the new Cabinet appointments with me. (*He goes to the chair* R *of the desk and puts down his briefcase*)

Eva Somehow I doubt it.

Turnbull I beg your pardon?

Eva He has become very decisive recently, he seems to have some opinions of his own.

Turnbull (*put out*) But as deputy PM he's bound to consult me.

Eva (*shrugging and smiling*) Maybe you're right . . .

   Gerry enters from the retiring room

Ah, Randolph. Ray is waiting for you.

Gerry Good-afternoon, Ray. What beautiful flowers, Eva. Thank you.

Eva I won't interrupt. See you later.

She exits smiling through the door to the hall

Gerry Now what can I do for you? (*He crosses to the desk and sits*)

Turnbull I thought we should discuss the Cabinet appointments. I presume you will have given the matter great thought, since our discussion last week.

Gerry Oh . . . er . . . yes . . . of course.

Turnbull (*producing a sheet of paper*) Here are my suggestions.

Gerry (*glancing briefly at the names*) I see you feel you should move from the Foreign Office to Number Eleven.

Turnbull (*miffed*) We discussed that only last week, Randolph.

Gerry (*easily*) Yes . . . but since then I've been giving the matter further thought. I am not sure it is a good idea . . .

Turnbull (*trying to conceal his anger*) But if I don't become Chancellor— what else are you offering?

Gerry Northern Ireland . . .

Turnbull What!

Gerry (*smiling*) It was a joke, Ray. You'll just have to leave it to me for a bit. I feel the whole place needs a good shake-up. Let's face it—your record at the Foreign Office has not been too impressive. We're only just recovering from Gibraltar and here you are buggering up the Virgin Islands.

Turnbull (*on his dignity*) Am I to understand that you are reneging on the arrangement we made?

Gerry (*with a charming smile*) Yes, I probably am. I'll need a few days to sort things out. Then we can discuss it more fully.

Turnbull Since you're making jokes about Ireland, perhaps you would enlighten me as to any change in attitude to the bill which is high on our priority list?

Gerry Yes, of course.

Pause

Turnbull You're not changing your mind about restricting the privileges accorded to the citizens of Eire, voting, social security, etc.

Gerry (*lost*) I see no reason to alter my previous attitude.

Turnbull You realize the international repercussions could be tremendous?

Gerry Er . . . yes, naturally I do.

Turnbull They're partners in the EEC . . .!

Gerry (*finding a fact at last*) But not allies in NATO.

Turnbull (*after a pause*) Quite. But after the latest bombings are you going to instigate immigration controls?

Gerry Public opinion demands it.

Turnbull Yes. As you appear to be in a changing mood, I just wanted to be sure ... (*Hard*) Think very carefully before you make any irrevocable decisions about me.

Gerry Oh, I will!

Turnbull I won't be blackmailed by you again.

Gerry (*interested*) Blackmailed?

Turnbull We won't go into that now. Don't forget, a week is a long time in politics, Randolph.

Gerry What an interesting comment. Actually this last week has absolutely flown by. Good-afternoon.

Turnbull opens the door to the hall

Frances enters from the hall, bumping into Turnbull

Frances Oh, I'm so sorry ... I er ...

Turnbull exits without apologizing

(*Surprised by Turnbull's manner, looking at Gerry*) Trouble?

Gerry You could say that.

Frances What's the matter? (*She closes the door firmly and moves* DS *of the desk to face it*)

Gerry Apparently he's been promised the house next door. I told him I'd changed my mind.

Frances Good God! You can't do that. I have no time for Turnbull (*an amused thought*)—in fact I would probably have enjoyed the scene—but please remember exactly who you are.

Gerry According to Her Majesty—who was extremely gracious by the way—I am the man whom she has invited to form the next government. She also advised me not to back her horse in the two-thirty this afternoon.

Frances You're beginning to believe your own publicity.

Gerry Aren't you pleased with my performance?

Frances Very. You've performed miracles—but I don't think we should ... er ... (*She moves to the round table*)

Gerry Push our luck?

Frances Exactly.

Gerry Pity. I am beginning to enjoy it. (*He scribbles on a page which he pushes towards her*) I am really getting into the part. I can even sign "Randolph Bolton" perfectly and without hesitation ... and with my right hand.

Frances (*studying the paper*) Impressive. Gerry, we've achieved our objective. The party is back in power. It would be fatal if anything went wrong now. You must quietly return to being Gerry Jackson and Bolton's body must be discovered—by a suitably doctored doctor.

Gerry (*sadly*) I suppose you're right. There are new pitfalls every hour—and I've been lucky. It's amazing how everyone accepts me.

Frances That's because, so far, there has been no reason not to. It must have been difficult with Eva. (*She sits in the chair* L *of the table*)

Gerry Er ... yes, that could have been very tricky. It was fortunate that the relationship was so ... cold.

Frances And what about your private secretary?

Gerry Oh yes, you might have warned me about Nigel.

Frances (*obnoxiously*) Did he suspect?

Gerry He suspects a certain coolness has developed in our relationship. This morning he said in an aggrieved tone that I hadn't kissed him for a week!

Frances Oh, dear. I didn't know about *him*.

Gerry Mr Bolton was a very busy fellow. I think it's time there were several changes made.

Frances (*sharply, standing and moving back to the desk*) That will not be up to you. I am meeting Dick Marr in a few minutes to finalize the plan but we'll be back here in half an hour. Please avoid any unnecessary contact. Stay here and keep quiet.

There is a knock at the hall door

Gerry Come in.

Nigel enters from the hall carrying a correspondence book with letters for signature

Nigel (*to Frances*) Good-afternoon, Minister. I'm not interrupting am I, sir? I need your signature on this letter.

Gerry Of course—excuse me a moment, Frances.

Nigel places the book in front of Gerry. He glances at the windows as Gerry reads the first letter

Frances I was just leaving anyway.

Gerry (*reading*) Don't rush away.

Nigel The nights are drawing in now. I'll give you some more light, Prime Minister. (*He moves to the door and switches on the lights*)

As he reads, Gerry casually picks up a pen in his left hand, while Nigel closes the curtains

Frances Well, I'm off. (*She sees Gerry signing with his left hand. She speaks sharply*) Prime Minister.

Gerry looks up and meets Frances' penetrating look. He is puzzled for a second as she somehow indicates the left hand. He understands and looks to see if Nigel has noticed

Gerry (*casually transferring the pen to his right hand*) Right! ... er ... Frances, I'll see you later ...

Frances I will be back as soon as I can.

She hesitates then exits to the hall

Gerry reads and signs one more letter then offers the book to Nigel

Gerry Thank you, Nigel.

Nigel (*collecting the book and hovering*) Is there anything else you want, Randolph?

Gerry (*firmly*) No thank you, Nigel. That will be all.

Nigel (*disappointed*) Very well then . . . (*He moves to the hall door and is about to say something as there is a noise outside*)

Eva opens the door and comes in

Eva I am sorry. I thought you were alone, Randolph. I wanted to discuss the arrangements for dinner tonight.

Gerry (*sitting up*) Of course. Nigel was just leaving, weren't you?

Nigel holds the door for her

Nigel Yes.

He smiles at her, hesitates, and exits

Gerry closes the door and looks at Eva — who comes into his arms. They kiss passionately

Gerry Frances is fascinated to know how I managed to deceive you.

Eva I am sure she is. Silly woman. She didn't notice your mistake. You looked at me with interest.

Gerry I know. I couldn't help it, you are a very attractive woman.

Eva And you are much too charming.

Gerry It is fortunate that Randolph and you had agreed to divorce after the election.

Eva Quite frankly I hated him. I am a very Merry Widow. I have enjoyed being married to you for three days.

Gerry (*smiling*) You are an unexpected bonus.

Eva Thank you. I'm glad we didn't waste too much time getting to know one another.

Gerry Was it only my "interest" that gave me away?

Eva No — after years of paralysing predictability you broke the pattern in several ways.

Gerry How?

Eva Not only did you *not* wake me up to ask if I was asleep, you also failed to gargle *Land of Hope and Glory*.

Gerry Did he really do that?

Eva Occasionally he varied it with selections from Gilbert and Sullivan.

Gerry Nobody briefed me on those little foibles.

Eva And you didn't disappear behind *The Times* at breakfast, you actually spoke to me.

Gerry I never could resist a captive audience.

Eva So I decided to take the initiative.

Gerry When I came out of the bathroom wearing nothing but a towel and found you waiting in my bed . . .

Eva You looked quite shocked.

Gerry Oh no — surprised certainly. I thought the game was up.

Eva (*innocently*) Was that why you threw in the towel so quickly?

They laugh and embrace

Gerry The pressure is on for me to step aside.

Eva They must be getting worried. (*She breaks away thoughtfully*) Has it ever occurred to you not to leave?

Gerry What? You mean stay on as Prime Minister? (*He breaks from her and moves* DSL. *He laughs*) Appoint the Cabinet: make speeches in the house: change the face of British politics?

Eva (*laughing*) Why not? You could get rid of all those creepy people.

Gerry It's a wonderful idea. Impractical. I'm afraid—I couldn't get away with it for long.

Eva You could if I briefed you very carefully. We could invent some illness to keep you out of the way while you studied all the problems and procedures. (*She moves* DS *to join him*)

Gerry Darling Eva! You're priceless! It's almost worth doing it for the laughs.

Eva So what could happen to you if you're found out now?

Gerry They'd probably throw me in the tower and cut my head off. (*A serious thought*) I wouldn't trust Dick Marr not to do something very nasty if he was pushed. (*He breaks* US *and around the desk*)

Eva They could hardly let it come out in the open. Can you imagine the headlines? (*She chuckles*) They'd all look such fools.

Gerry (*serious but smiling*) No, they wouldn't leak it to Robin Day or David Frost. I believe they would deal with me in a more final way.

Eva (*going to him*) You mean they'd kill you.

Gerry (*serious*) I'm sure of it.

Eva Don't be silly. You're letting your thespian background influence you. (*Trying to convince herself*) The media would have a field day. You'd be on all the chat shows. Prime time for the Prime Pretender.

Gerry (*shaking his head*) I'd like to think that's how it would be—a few weeks in prison and masses of publicity; offers of parts from the Royal Shakespeare Company to *Jackanory*. But I'm afraid this is not a game to the people involved. They wouldn't be embarrassed, they'd be mortified. They would stop at nothing to protect themselves. You can shout at politicians, insult them, revile them, accuse them—but *never* laugh at them. (*He moves* DS *to Eva*)

Eva (*kissing him*) If you really believe that, darling, then I suggest you retire from public life with some haste.

Gerry I'm afraid you're right. You mustn't forget the amount of people already involved—most of them unwittingly. M.I.5, Cabinet Ministers, Party Workers, the Queen. I've even given brief interviews to the press. If it comes out they will all be left with a great deal of egg on their faces.

Eva Yes, mind you I have admired the way you've done it. (*She sits in the chair* L *of the table*)

Gerry Well even small-part actors have to cope with the press from time to time. I've always been good at ad-libbing.

Eva I wonder why you've not been more successful as an actor—you're obviously very talented?

Gerry (*shrugging*) The wrong time and the wrong place. (*After a pause*) And now, finally, this. The best part I've ever had and I can't even capitalize on it. It's like the rabbi who played golf on a Saturday and holed in one. Who could he tell?

Eva (*sympathetically*) When I'm an official widow and you are Gerry Jackson again maybe we will find something much better together than playing at politics.

They look into each other's eyes and kiss gently. There is a knock on the door and Gerry moves back to his desk

Gerry Come in.

Dick Marr enters from the hall

Eva Good-evening, Dick.
Dick Good-evening, er ... Randolph, Eva. Nigel said to come straight in.
Gerry Yes. Come in, Dick. I was expecting you. Is Frances not with you?
Dick She is on her way, she——
Eva (*interrupting*) Oh Dick, I must congratulate you on your increased majority. (*She stands and moves* US *to Dick*)
Dick Thank you, Eva.
Eva It must be so uncomfortable having to sit on a marginal seat.

Dick nods

But it seems my husband has the country behind him.
Dick (*abruptly*) Of course.
Eva I was reading this morning's newspapers – several had editorials about the personal influence that Randolph has on the electorate. (*She sits on the fender* US)
Dick (*uncomfortably*) We are only too well aware of that, Eva, and grateful ...
Eva (*needling*) It would be interesting to see what would happen to the party should anything ever happen to him.

Dick looks sharply at Gerry who is listening with some amusement

Gerry Stop teasing, Eva. Nothing's going to happen to me, is it, Dick?
Dick Of course not.
Gerry There you are, Eva. I'm in good hands. What could be safer than the protection of the Home Office?
Eva (*ingenuously*) But that was in the old Cabinet, Randolph.
Dick (*sharply*) What does that mean?
Gerry Nothing – yet. I had a brief meeting with Ray. I suggested that a reshuffle might be necessary, and——
Dick (*trying not to explode in front of Eva*) A reshuffle? I think it's time we had a serious discussion. (*He moves to the desk*)
Gerry Yes. I thought you would.

The buzzer sounds and Gerry answers it

  Yes? ... Right, Nigel. ... No, ask him to wait. ... You can send her up. ... Thank you. (*He replaces the phone*) Frances is here and Ray is waiting. Any moment now we can have an Inner Cabinet meeting (*he turns to Eva*) and then I am afraid I will have to ask you to leave, my dear.
Eva Would you like me to go *now*, Randolph? (*She stands*)

Gerry No hurry.

Dick fumes. There is a knock on the door

Come in.

Frances enters from the hall

(*Smiling*) Welcome back.

Frances (*looking pointedly at Eva*) Prime Minister, we have several important issues to discuss and a few matters to settle *before* Ray Turnbull comes
up.

Gerry You can speak freely in front of Eva.

Frances I don't think that would be in order.

Eva Really, Frances! (*She crosses to the armchair and sits*) Did you really
think you could fool *me*?

Dick and Frances look at her in silence

Dick Fool you? What do you mean, Eva? — No-one is trying to——

Frances Shut up, Dick! She knows. (*After a pause*) Why haven't you said
anything, Eva? (*She crosses to Eva*)

Eva I have my reasons.

Dick (*moving to join Eva and Frances*) Whatever they are it is immaterial. The
point is this deception has gone on long enough. As we agreed the time has
come for Jackson to resume his acting career. The financial arrangements
have been honoured. It is time to shock the nation by announcing the
untimely death of the Prime Minister.

Eva And I shall have great sympathy.

Frances You deserve it.

Eva (*drily*) For putting up with him for twenty years.

Frances Absolutely. Now we have to arrange the details.

Dick I've discussed it with Hardacre and told him we will be needing the
body so he's standing by.

Eva Does Hardacre know everything?

Frances Good heavens, no. He believes the real Randolph is a Russian spy
and we have some devious plan to embarrass the CIA.

Gerry Why the CIA?

Dick The more confused the better — and it's hard to find anything more
confused than the CIA.

Eva Before I leave you to your detailed plots I shall put a small thought into
your heads. (*She stands and crosses to the desk*)

Dick (*abruptly*) Yes, Eva. What is it?

Eva Might it not be a good idea to arrange the Cabinet reshuffle to suit
yourselves — while you still have some control over the situation.

Dick (*thoughtfully*) She has a point, Frances.

Frances Yes, but every minute we risk exposure. But if Turnbull gets elected
as leader then everything will have been for nothing.

Gerry Not everything — the party is back in power.

Frances How long would it be before we could announce the Cabinet
appointments?

Dick Good God. (*Indicating Gerry*) He's got to interview everyone. Make them an offer, wait for their answers, discuss their problems. We haven't time to brief him.

Frances (*smiling for the first time*) He's done pretty well so far and he's even indicated to Ray that he's not going to be made Chancellor.

Dick (*amazed*) He's *what?*

Frances It's true.

Dick (*incredulous*) How did he react?

Gerry (*intervening*) Not too well I admit. In fact I think an accurate description would be apoplectic. (*He raises an enquiring eyebrow to Frances*)

Frances (*nodding*) He's furious especially at being excluded from this meeting. He's downstairs browbeating Nigel now.

Dick (*to Gerry*) Why did you do it? You had no authority. I never gave permission . . .

Gerry (*handing him the paper that Turnbull left*) He gave me his "suggestions". I thought he needed deflating a little.

Dick (*reading*) Good God! He wants Number Eleven and I'm to be moved to (*furious*) Ag and Fish!

Frances (*snatching the paper*) He's left me with the Arts. I've got to have Environment. Randolph promised.

They are both furious. There is a brief pause

Eva (*calmly*) Perhaps if you ask nicely and behave like good children, my husband might arrange it . . . (*She crosses* DS *and sits in the chair by the window*)

They turn and stare at her and then at Gerry as the buzzer goes and Gerry answers

Gerry Yes? . . . I see. (*He replaces the receiver*) You have about thirty seconds to make up your minds. Nigel couldn't hold back Turnbull any longer.

Dick (*through gritted teeth*) I'd like you to fire the bastard.

Frances Throw him out of the government altogether.

Eva Why don't you offer him Education?

Dick Don't be silly, the stupid sod can't read . . .

The hall door is thrown open and Turnbull storms in

Gerry (*charming*) Hello, Ray. So sorry to keep you waiting——

Turnbull (*red in the face*) How dare you behave like this to me, Randolph?

Gerry Would you prefer this discussion in private?

Turnbull (*shouting*) I don't give a damn who hears. If you don't honour your promise to me I shall see to it you are removed as leader of the party.

Gerry (*calmly*) Honour? I didn't know that word still existed in political vocabulary.

Turnbull Don't get sarcastic with me — if I have to I'll tell everyone about the deals you did — the compromises you made — the underhand bribes you paid. The honours you handed out. You needed me to become the leader — well by God! — you are not going to get rid of me without a fight.

Dick (*to Turnbull*) You haven't been too particular about who you would like to ditch.

Frances If you think I'm content to stay outside the Cabinet you are greatly mistaken. (*She waves the piece of paper*)

Turnbull (*shouting*) I don't have to take advice from either of you. (*To Gerry*) That paper was confidential.

The buzzer goes again and Gerry, who has been listening to the row with calm detachment, answers

Gerry Yes? . . . Ask him to wait. . . . That important? You'd better send him in. (*He replaces the receiver and speaks to the room in general*) Colonel Hardacre insists on seeing me on the most urgent security matter . . .

Turnbull He can wait.

Gerry I gather he can't. Maybe we've been invaded! There are other matters of some importance in the world, besides your personal problems, Turnbull.

Eva stifles a giggle as there is a knock on the door to the hall

Come in.

Colonel Hardacre enters from the hall

Colonel I . . . er . . . have something of vital importance to tell you, Prime Minister.

Gerry Go ahead, Colonel. These are all trusted associates.

Colonel I am sorry, sir. I must make my report to you personally. If after that you wish to inform the others that is, of course, your decision.

Gerry shrugs and looks at them expectantly. They are all reluctant to leave — for their various reasons

Gerry Would you mind withdrawing for a few minutes, please?

Eva stands and crosses to the hall door

Turnbull Before I go I must insist that we have a full Cabinet meeting tonight.

Eva (*sweetly*) I was under the impression that the new Cabinet had not been appointed yet.

Turnbull (*irritated*) I was referring to the inner circle — the senior members. You know exactly who I mean.

Eva Ahh!

She exits

Turnbull glares after her then at Gerry

Gerry I see no objection. How do you feel, Dick, Frances?

Dick I . . . er . . . well . . . I suppose . . .

Frances (*bitterly*) I am not senior enough to argue.

Gerry (*grandly*) I feel that position might change, Frances, in the near future.

Turnbull Nine o'clock sharp, then; I'll tell Nigel to inform everyone.

He exits — followed by Dick and Frances, to the hall

Gerry Well, Colonel? I gather the matter is extremely important.

Colonel Yes, sir. (*He is uneasy*)

Gerry Well go on man, spit it out.

Colonel Sir! It concerns the ringer, sir.

Gerry (*not understanding*) Ringer?

Colonel *Your* ringer — the foreign agent.

Gerry (*dawning and apprehensive*) Ah! Of course. The dead ringer ... well?

Colonel You were under the impression that he died of a heart attack.

Gerry (*uncertainly*) Yes.

Colonel I regret to inform you, sir, that was not correct. He was poisoned.

Gerry (*after a beat*) You mean he was *murdered*?

Colonel That would appear highly probable, sir.

CURTAIN

ACT II

SCENE 1

The same. A few moments later

The positions are the same. Gerry sits behind the desk—deep in thought. The Colonel stands. Perhaps Gerry has swivelled his chair so he looks away

Gerry (*swivelling to face Hardacre*) You are absolutely sure he was poisoned?

Colonel Absolutely, sir. The substance is called: Ricin. (*Spelling it out*) R-I-C-I-N.

Gerry Ricin?

Colonel Yes. It is very difficult to detect and can give the same symptoms as a heart attack.

Gerry I see. Do sit down.

Colonel (*after a pause, sitting in the chair R of the desk*) You realize that as no-one appears to know he was a ringer—you, Prime Minister, were the intended victim.

Gerry (*nodding*) It had dawned on me. (*To himself*) I should be paid danger money.

Colonel (*without humour*) It's the job probably, sir—nothing personal.

Gerry Thank you, that thought consoles me. How was he poisoned?

Colonel The poison could have been swallowed or administered. A pinprick is all that is needed.

Gerry Like the Hungarian broadcaster?

Colonel Exactly. He was Bulgarian actually. The full post-mortem will give us more information.

Gerry (*sharply*) Post-mortem—who gave permission for that?

Colonel (*stiffly*) It is normal procedure. No-one told me not to——

Gerry (*angrily*) You have exceeded your authority, Colonel. We were anticipating using the body. You were told to keep it on ice.

Colonel (*stiffly*) Do I understand that M.I.6 were to be involved . . . without my knowledge? This is counter-espionage, my department has the authority——

Gerry I am not prepared to discuss that but it certainly changes my plans.

Colonel I apologize if I have made a mistake, sir. Your safety is my prime concern. (*Ruefully*) There are so many moles being unearthed, extreme caution must be exercised. It's difficult to trust anybody.

Gerry I just hope I can trust you.

Colonel Implicitly . . . but then I would say that if I was a mole, wouldn't I?

Gerry (*smiling ruefully*) Yes, of course. This whole thing is beginning to feel like an episode from *Toad of Toad Hall*. But who are Badger and Ratty and who is the Chief Weasel?

Colonel (*almost a joke*) I presume you are the Toad, sir. (*He coughs*) As none of my people were aware of the ringer — it's probably one of yours.

Gerry Are you implying that one of my close associates is a killer?

Colonel I have done some checking up. During the course of the evening many people were in and out of this room — including your wife, your private secretary, Mr Turnbull, Mr Marr and Mrs Crowdray. Also a Mr Jackson was checked in and shown up — I presume on your authority.

Gerry (*after a moment's pause*) Mrs Cowdray was expecting a Mr Jackson — a PR person — he never arrived here.

Colonel (*pleased*) And he was not checked out. There's your ringer, sir.

Gerry For heaven's sake, isn't there some other word you could use? It sounds like an American movie — about switching racehorses.

Colonel I must repeat you are in danger. I intend to investigate the matter thoroughly.

Gerry But *discreetly*, Colonel Hardacre. There is no proof and we must avoid a scandal. You cannot go around accusing Ministers of the Crown ... unless you have proof, of course.

Colonel I shall get it. You can rely on me.

Gerry On this business you will report to me personally.

Colonel Yes, sir. (*He stands*)

Gerry (*thoughtfully*) I presume your men who moved the body and the medical team are completely trustworthy?

Colonel Absolutely, sir.

Gerry They didn't see the likeness?

Colonel They did not comment and I thought it best not to emphasize the point.

Gerry Well, I hope you are right — but kindly ensure there is no leak at all.

Colonel Do I gather you had hoped to use the body to embarrass the other side in some way?

Gerry (*devious*) There was some scheme under consideration.

Colonel (*sniffing*) It sounds more like a CIA operation.

Gerry (*looking as if there could be something in this*) Sorry I can't discuss that any further, Colonel Hardacre.

Colonel (*disgruntled*) I quite understand, sir.

Gerry When you have completed the post-mortem you may then see that there is no further trace of the body.

Colonel Leave it to me, Prime Minister.

Gerry (*glancing at his watch*) Well, I think I need a drink. (*He gets up and goes to the drinks cabinet*) What about you?

Colonel No, thank you, sir.

Gerry (*picking up the rum bottle with some distaste*) I suppose you are on duty.

Colonel (*sharply*) Don't touch that! (*He moves to Gerry*)

Gerry What?

Colonel I know you enjoy your rum, sir. Does anyone else drink it?

Gerry No — as a matter of fact it is not that popular ...

Colonel Have you used it since the night in question?

Gerry (*thoughtfully*) No.

Colonel (*producing a handkerchief*) Then I shall take this with me, sir, and have it analysed.

Gerry Good heavens! (*Sniffing the bottle nervously and handing it over*) In that case I'll have a small Scotch. Now, Colonel, I intend to ask the others to return and put them in the picture.

Colonel Are you sure that's wise, sir—they are all suspects.

Gerry It will give you a chance to observe their reactions.

Colonel (*nodding*) Right.

Gerry moves back to the desk, presses the buzzer and lifts the receiver

Gerry Nigel?... Yes, would you ask my wife and the gang of three to return, please?... I see.... Right, the others then.... Thank you. (*He replaces the receiver*) Mr Turnbull has left. Make yourself comfortable, Hardacre. (*He indicates a chair by the window*)

The Colonel sits, holding the rum bottle in his handkerchief. He then puts it in his briefcase. Gerry sits at his desk and sips his drink. He calls "Come in" when there is a knock on the door

Eva, Frances and Dick enter from the hall

Eva Are you sure you want me, Randolph? If it's official business perhaps I should ...?

Gerry Please sit down, Eva. The information Colonel Hardacre has given me is something you should all hear.

Eva sits R of the deak, Frances and Dick either side of the round table. They are all anxiously hanging on his words

I should emphasize that what I have to say is for your ears only.

Dick (*impatiently*) Yes, yes, please go on.

Gerry (*after a pause—well aware of the tension*) With the exception of Hardacre's department—we five people in this room are meant to be the *only* ones who know of the look-alike, double ... call him what you will, and the Colonel always refers to him as a "ringer".

Frances Yes, yes. Well?

Gerry (*enjoying the drama*) Well, it appears that this ringer—a supposed Russian agent—did not die of a heart attack when he was discovered as we imagined.

There is a significant pause

He was *murdered*.

He looks at them—as does the Colonel. They portray varying emotions of surprise and shock and concern

Eva (*shocked*) Murdered?

Gerry Colonel ...

Colonel Purely by chance the "ringer" was killed ... he was poisoned. It is safe to assume that the Prime Minister was the intended target.

There is a pause

Gerry Thank you, Colonel. You may proceed as we discussed.
Colonel (*rising and going to the hall door*) Thank you, sir.

He exits to the hall

Gerry So there you have it . . . at least the Colonel's version of events, and I should explain that the Colonel is adamant that you are all prime suspects.

They stare in astonishment

And perhaps I should add that I completely agree with him!
Dick (*exploding*) Look here, Jackson—that is ridiculous. Why on earth should I have any reason to kill the Prime Minister?
Gerry You had the opportunity and the motive.
Dick That's nonsense.
Frances (*interrupting*) What motive?
Gerry (*holding a bunch of keys*) By way of researching my part as quickly and thoroughly as I could, I read the contents of this drawer. I understand only Randolph had the key. The contents proved fascinating. (*He replaces the keys in his jacket pocket*)
Frances (*frustrated and angry*) Oh! Do stop dramatizing, Gerry! Say what you have to say.
Gerry (*relaxed*) Let me enjoy my little moment, Frances. This is a dimension that I had not anticipated . . . and for which I believe I have not been adequately compensated. (*He stands and moves* DL *around the desk*)
Dick Are you trying to blackmail me into paying you more money?
Gerry Money was never my main interest. For me the fascination was the challenge.
Frances *What* was in the drawer?
Gerry (*smiling at her*) A list of intended Cabinet appointments and various notes on personalities and policies. The media would probably sell their souls for those few handwritten pages.
Eva (*quietly*) Any *personal* comments.
Gerry (*gently*) Surprisingly, dear Eva, you are not mentioned at all.
Eva Perhaps I should be grateful for that.
Frances (*to Gerry*) For God's sake get on with it!
Gerry It appears that Dick and Randolph had a serious disagreement over various policy matters.
Dick (*uncomfortably*) We did not see eye to eye on a special police unit that I was forming.
Gerry A para-military force is how he described it. Be that as it may—you were not going to be offered the Home Office again. I think you had an inkling of this.
Dick (*coldly*) I don't believe you.
Gerry It is a fact and there is the clear motive. You were going to be forced to resign. I do not believe life on the back benches is attractive to you.
Dick This is all nonsense. Frances, we cannot allow this charade to go on. Jackson has served his purpose, he must go.
Frances One moment, Dick. Before we decide on the best course of action, I'd like to see those papers.

Gerry (*shaking his head*) Sorry but no. They are part of my insurance
policy—that and a brief but explicit account of recent events which I have
written down and lodged, in a sealed envelope of course, with a certain
reliable party. That party will do what is necessary if physical harm should
come to me—that is, the Prime Minister. (*He pauses*) So it is in all your
interests to keep me alive.

Dick I knew we couldn't trust him, Frances. Look at the mess you've got
us into.

Gerry I've heard that line before.

Frances (*standing*) Don't blame it all on me. Apart from your total co-
operation *and* financial backing, it appears you have a great deal more to
gain—or lose than I have. Tell me, Gerry—what was in that drawer that
refers to me?

Gerry You don't seem to have done too badly. He was going to offer you
Education—in return for which he would demand complete loyalty on
certain issues. Of course, I don't know *exactly* what those issues were——

Frances (*too quickly*) Nothing important. (*She breaks* DR)

Dick (*sharply*) So you say.

Frances Dick, do you really think I killed him?

Dick (*standing and crossing to her*) I did not say that, but *you* diagnosed a
heart attack and suggested we use Jackson. You had the same opportunity
and possibly motive as me. Anyway, this is stupid—if it was done by
someone near to him it is far more likely to be Turnbull.

Frances Or Eva.

They both turn to face her

Eva I was wondering when you'd get round to me. But I had no motive. We'd
agreed to divorce after the election—I would create no scandal in return
for a comfortable financial settlement. You see—no problems—no
motive.

Frances We only have your word for that.

Eva You could verify it with the solicitors.

Dick (*turning to face Frances*) The most obvious person to benefit from
Randolph's death is Ray Turnbull.

Frances Yes, that's right. He was here twice that night . . . was the second
time to check up?

Eva He would inevitably have taken over as leader.

Frances (*thinking*) But when he saw Randolph on the bed, he assumed he
was sleeping.

Dick That was probably a very clever bluff.

Gerry Then he must have been a bit surprised to have found me alive. He
certainly hid it well.

Eva Is it not possible that it was someone else? A third party, not one of us at
all.

Gerry It would be more comfortable to think so.

Dick (*moving to the desk*) What about his private secretary, Nigel?

Gerry (*drily*) And what was his motive—jealousy? We will have to wait for
(*pause*) the pathologist's report.

Frances Are they doing a post-mortem?

Gerry nods

Dick (*shocked*) Who gave permission? That ruins everything. We can hardly
prop the body up behind a desk and claim he had a heart attack now.
Frances (*anxiously*) You're right. It changes everything.
Eva It certainly does. If Gerry disappears now there will be a tremendous
hue and cry. The security services of the world will be involved.
Dick (*very worried*) And we'd have to let Hardacre in on the truth ...
Frances And how would he react?
Gerry (*easily*) He'd be so embarrassed at being wrong again—he'd probably
have a heart attack.
Dick There is no need for flippancy, Jackson.
Gerry I suggest you continue to address me as Randolph for the time being.
Frances (*coming to a decision*) You must stay on, the alternative is disastrous.
It will give us time to formulate a foolproof plan. Dick?
Dick (*reluctantly*) I agree, though God knows how much longer he can get
away with it.

Eva stands and moves DR *to join Dick and Frances*

Eva I've already suggested a mild illness. Overwork—he has to take a short
break.
Frances Good idea. We'll announce it after the meeting tonight. In the
meantime we'll make a timetable and continue a cramming course for
Gerry.

They are talking among themselves

Gerry I am a quick study.
Dick First of all there are the leading personalities—their names and
interests and——
Eva Then there is parliamentary procedure, "My Honourable Friend" and
the "Right Honourable Lady", etc. Randolph would never get that wrong.
What happens when Gerry has to attend Question Time in the House ...?
Dick God forbid! It would be a disaster.
Eva Knowing Gerry he'd say something.
Gerry "To be, or not to be." Now I come to think of it, that *is* the question.
Dick Exactly. The first priority is choosing the new government. That will be
the main items on tonight's agenda. Frances and I will let you know what
to do and who to appoint. We'll draw up a list.
Gerry (*with irony*) And to hell with collective Cabinet decisions. I shall be
interested to see it—especially the jobs you take for yourselves.
Frances We will be your left and right hand.
Eva (*drily*) And you know the old saying—never let your left hand know
what your right hand is doing. (*She moves* DL *to sit in the chair by the
window*)
Gerry (*laughing*) Do I take it that you all wish me to extend my engagement?
Dick } (*together*) { Of course.
Frances } { Definitely.

Eva (*smiling*) You've got my vote, too. Darling, don't you think you should check with your theatrical agent?

Gerry (*smiling*) Renegotiate my contract? (*He sees Dick's face*) Perhaps not. But I should make a short visit to Switzerland for my health. Don't you agree, Dick?

Dick (*disgruntled*) You will find everything in order. (*He gets up to leave with Frances*) And don't forget, you've already had a down-payment.

Gerry (*stopping him*) I know it's running a risk but I have an idea that a brief act from me at the beginning of tonight's meeting would help.

Frances What do you mean?

Gerry Come and get me, Frances, once they are all seated. That way I can bring the meeting to order without having to exchange any personal remarks. I shall then give my "turning pale and looking ill" performance and retire. Later you can announce I've been ordered to rest. Nobody will query it.

Dick True. And we'll have the time we need to find a solution. Right, that's agreed.

The intercom buzzes. Gerry answers

Gerry Yes, Nigel? ... (*He suddenly sits up and listens intently*) I see. ... What do you mean exactly? ... No, don't speak to anyone until you've talked to me. ... NOBODY! Is that understood? ... Yes. ... Come and see me when you've finished. (*He replaces the receiver thoughtfully*)

The others wait anxiously

Dick Well—what was that all about?

Frances You look worried ...

Eva What is it?

Gerry I'm not quite sure. Nigel is obviously in a state.

Dick What about?

Gerry He wouldn't say on the house phone—except that it is a massive security problem. He thought he should speak to Hardacre.

Frances You dissuaded him, of course.

Gerry nods

Dick (*hard*) Does he *know*?

Gerry (*shrugging*) I don't think so—not everything anyway, otherwise why would he call *me*?

Eva You'd better get him in quickly and find out.

Gerry (*strained*) We mustn't show any signs of worry or panic. He's trapped with the general secretary of the Boilermakers' Union—I've told him to come in when he's gone. (*He looks at them calmly then speaks with authority*) Leave it to me. I'll find out what's going on and let you know.

Dick and Frances exchange a look and she nods. Dick opens the door to the hall

Frances exits

Dick Good-night ... er ... Randolph.

Dick exits to the hall, looking worried

Eva stands, moves to the drinks cabinet and refills his glass

Eva You know you handled that very well. I believe you'll make a good Prime Minister.

Gerry Thank you, Eva, but I have to admit I am beginning to feel the strain. (*He takes off his jacket and drops it over the chair behind the desk*)

Eva Don't worry too much about Nigel—he's always getting in a tizzy about something.

Gerry I'll try not to ... someone's probably pinched the paper clips.

Eva Relax. Have a drink. I have a lovely meal prepared for you. It will be ready in an hour.

Gerry (*kissing her lightly*) That will be nice, darling.

Eva I'll see you later.

Gerry exits through the retiring room door

Eva hesitates for a second, then takes the bunch of keys from his jacket pocket and goes to the desk. She tries desperately to find the right key for the drawer. She opens the drawer

Gerry quietly opens the retiring room door and unseen, watches for a moment

Gerry What a pity, my darling.

Eva starts guiltily

I was hoping you were the one person I could trust.

The hall door bursts open and Nigel rushes in almost hysterical

Nigel I've got to talk to you!

Gerry What on earth?

Nigel It's terribly urgent——

Gerry (*angrily*) Not now, Nigel. Eva, we must——

Eva (*moving to the door to the hall*) Our discussion can wait——

Gerry No it can't——

Nigel (*very upset*) You've got to listen!

Eva I'll talk to you later, Randolph.

She exits to the hall

Gerry hurries after her

Nigel Randolph!

Gerry (*as he exits*) For God's sake shut up, Nigel! Eva—I demand an explanation ...

Gerry exits to the hall

Nigel is distraught. He takes an envelope from his pocket

Nigel I just hope you read this before it's too late. (*He places the envelope on the desk. He looks anxiously at his watch and then sees the drawer open, looks quickly towards the door and then starts to read a paper which he lifts out*)

A hand comes round the door and flicks off the lights

We hear Nigel gasp and catch the faint silhouette of a figure coming into the room

Who's that? ... Put the lights on!

There is a noise of a faint scuffle

W-what are you doing? ... Who are you?

There is another gasp

Then perhaps we catch a momentary glimpse of a figure slipping out of the door

There is silence for a few seconds then the door is opened fully and Gerry is silhouetted in the doorway. He reaches out and switches on the lights

Nigel is slumped over the desk – apparently dead. Gerry walks over to the desk as——

the CURTAIN *falls*

SCENE 2

The same. Evening, three weeks later.

The room is empty; there is a knock on the hall door and from the retiring room Gerry calls out "Come in"

Turnbull enters from the hall

Turnbull Good-evening, Prime Minister ... Oh! Randolph?
Gerry (*off*) Come in, Ray. Am I expecting you?
Turnbull No. I just wanted a few words with you.
Gerry (*off*) I won't be a minute. Make yourself comfortable.
Turnbull Thank you. No hurry.

While keeping an eye on the door Turnbull eases over to the desk to see if there is anything of interest. An open folder catches his eye and he peers closer and picks up a letter

Gerry (*off*) Oh Ray, there's an interesting despatch from our man in Washington.

Turnbull jumps guiltily and puts down the paper and breaks DL

It's on the desk. Why don't you read it?
Turnbull Er ... Oh! Yes. Thank you. (*He moves back to the desk and picks up the letter*)
Gerry (*off*) Oh, and help yourself to a drink.
Turnbull No thanks, I'm not much of a drinker nowadays. Can I get you your usual? Rum and tonic, isn't it?

Gerry (*off*) No thank you. I've gone off it, can't think why, I used to like it. Was there something special you wanted to talk about?

Turnbull Just a chat, and I wanted to congratulate you on your speech in the House yesterday. I've never known your timing so impeccable.

Gerry enters smiling

Gerry (*crossing to the desk*) Thank you. Yes, it did seem to go down rather well. Well what do you think of Washington's plan for the Middle East?

Turnbull (*handing back the letter*) We must be careful not to get drawn into the controversy. I must say you're looking much better for your enforced rest. I'm glad our little contretemps has resolved itself.

Gerry Yes, I really wasn't myself. I must have underestimated the strain of the election and then there was that dreadful business of Nigel's death which still remains unresolved.

Turnbull Yes, of course. You know, you and I go too far back to allow the occasional difference of opinion to spoil our relationship. Do you know, it's twenty years since you were the candidate at that by-election and I came up to support you.

Gerry (*lightly*) Time flies by as we get older – and the policemen get younger.

Turnbull I shall never forget that night after the election. You and I dined together at the *Saracen's Head*. (*Reminiscing*) We both got very drunk and the landlord had to drive us home at three in the morning.

Gerry (*after a beat*) Quite a night.

Turnbull We settled the problems of the world.

Gerry It's easy at three in the morning. (*Changing the subject*) Have you settled in comfortably next door?

Turnbull Very. There are a few policy decisions I'd like to talk over. Did you have much trouble with Dick Marr?

Gerry (*nodding*) He was not at all keen to take Northern Ireland. (*He moves* DL *of the desk and sits on the corner*)

Turnbull (*chuckling*) I bet he wasn't. Did you have a row?

Gerry Not at all. I asked him which he preferred Northern Ireland or the back benches.

Turnbull (*laughing*) I hope he does a good job. And that he's thought through the political implications of withdrawing those two battalions.

Gerry Ray, I know he is not one of your favourite people but he is very clever.

Turnbull He's also very devious. Ambition is all very well provided it is tempered with the right political instincts.

Gerry Right for our side you mean. Don't worry, I'll keep a close watch on Dick Marr.

Turnbull Thank you. We are likely to have a great deal of trouble with the unions in the next round of pay talks. I don't want the issue clouded or negotiations marred ...

Gerry (*chuckling*) What a clever pun. (*He moves to the drinks cabinet*)

Turnbull (*unaware*) What?

Gerry Nothing.

Turnbull Don't forget, Prime Minister, he wants your job.

Gerry So does everyone . . . (*placatingly*) He'll be all right, I promise you.
Turnbull Hmm. Well—I hope you are right. I'm never quite sure where his first loyalty is. (*He gets up to leave*)
Gerry With Dick Marr of course.
Turnbull (*smiling*) I wished I'd seen his face when you said Northern Ireland or the back benches. (*He laughs and opens the door*)

Eva is about to enter

He stands aside and ushers her in

Good-evening, Eva. That husband of yours has a sense of humour—never noticed it before. Good-night, Prime Minister. (*As he exits, laughing*) Northern Ireland or the back benches, that's very good.

Turnbull exits

Eva (*closing the door with a surprised look*) I've never seen him smile before, let alone laugh. It must have been a good joke.

Gerry pours a drink and gives it to her

Gerry Not really—but it was at Dick's expense. (*Thoughtfully*) But you are right—he's up to something.
Eva I'm amazed you've placated Ray. And your performance in the House . . . how on earth have you done it?
Gerry (*moving back to the desk*) Those days I spent heavily disguised sitting in the Strangers' Gallery learning all the names and procedure. It's not too difficult once you get the hang of it. I've practically learnt Hansard by heart. Jollier than Ibsen but only just.
Eva I'm glad you've forgiven me for my snooping. (*She moves to the round table and sits in the DL chair*)
Gerry Completely. Your female curiosity got the better of you.
Eva I thought you were hiding something, some dreadful revelation that Randolph had written down about my past. There were one or two incidents I'd prefer to forget.
Gerry Well you saw the contents of the drawer. You know, I wasn't lying. (*Joking*) Unless of course, Olga, you are after all, a Russian mince pie?
Eva I am not the slightest bit interested in the notes on private conversations with other Heads of State.
Gerry If anyone knows you've ever seen those papers we'll both be for the chop. (*He moves down* C)
Eva My paranoid husband had the most extraordinary collection of highly confidential information on his intimate colleagues.
Gerry Surely that is not normal practice?
Eva I don't know, but it explains why he was always able to carry his Cabinet with such apparent unanimity.
Gerry I thought it was probably because of that most powerful piece of parliamentary legislation—the Old Pals Act.
Eva So did I. Now it seems it was just old-fashioned blackmail.
Gerry It is *incredible* that the scandal of Ultrasonic Marine Investments was hushed up.

Eva Exactly, Ultrasonic Marine was incredible.

Gerry Someone as we all know made a fortune out of that budget leak.

Eva (*standing, moving to him*) I agree. You have some very explosive material in your hands, Gerry, be careful how you use it.

Gerry I don't intend to touch it.

Eva You never know—it could be a vital safeguard.

Gerry I'll remember that. I'm sorry to bring this up again. It's not that I don't believe you but . . . well . . . what were those incidents in the past that you are so nervous about?

Eva Does it matter?

Gerry Perhaps it does.

Eva It was years ago.

Gerry Was it a lover?

Eva (*hesitating*) Yes.

Gerry That is not surprising in an unhappy marriage. But there was something else as well, wasn't there?

Eva Can't we trust each other?

Gerry We're all living some sort of lie. Dick, Frances, you, *me*.

Eva I trust *you*.

Gerry God knows why.

Eva How can I prove myself?

Gerry By telling me what actually happened.

Eva (*thinking for a moment*) I had a love affair—and Randolph found out.

Gerry Careless of you. (*He breaks upstage to the fender and sits*)

Eva Yes—but I was unlucky.

Gerry In what way?

Eva Randolph at that time became paranoic.

Gerry I'm beginning to understand how he felt.

Eva He was convinced that his life was in danger. (*She moves to sit on the fender next to Gerry*)

Gerry (*drily*) He was proved right.

Eva He kept changing his security people, he didn't trust even them. As for the Foreign Office he treated them as if they were a foreign country.

Gerry Well they are aren't they, Philby, Maclean, Burgess, I suppose an odd patriot slips in from time to time.

Eva He was obsessed with the CIA, the KGB and BOSS.

Gerry Boss?

Eva South African State Security.

Gerry Ah! Yes, of course. They are called DONS now.

Eva (*looking at him sharply*) Really? I didn't know you were so well briefed.

Gerry (*shrugging*) Department of National Security, DONS sounds more intellectual somehow—a stray piece of information that got lodged in a corner of my mind.

Eva I see. (*She stands and moves* DR) He had everyone near him investigated, screened, followed. Even Cabinet colleagues had their phones tapped.

Gerry And you got caught in the middle of the surveillance. (*He stands and moves to join her*)

Eva Exactly. I don't think Randolph cared a damn about my having an affair — unless I was indiscreet. Now you know the worst.

Gerry Do I?

Eva Everything that matters. Don't worry, I am not going to poison you.

Gerry (*lightly*) Well that is a great relief. I hope no-one else will. I have this itchy spot between my shoulder blades — waiting for the knife. (*He breaks* c)

Eva It would probably only be a needle. Don't worry, I'll help you to protect yourself.

They laugh and embrace

How much longer are you going to stay on?

Gerry Quite frankly I'm in no hurry to leave. Most people dream of what they would do if only they could be Prime Minister for a few days. This may be the only chance I have to do something worthwhile . . . I might even influence, in a small way, the course of events.

Eva Steady on, darling. Don't let it go to your head.

Gerry I'll try not to. You'll have to go in a moment. Dick and Frances have "requested" a private meeting. I've suggested they stay for dinner.

Eva Fine, but watch out for him. He's longing for the chance to get rid of you.

Gerry But he hasn't been able to work out a foolproof plan yet. There's not much either of them can do without implicating themselves.

Eva What about M.I.5? (*She moves to the drinks cabinet*)

Gerry Security is very tight but I've heard little from Hardacre — ever since he explained that the ringer had probably taken a suicide pill rather than risk questioning. It's an easy answer for Hardacre.

Eva A suicide pill . . . well, I hope he stays satisfied for your sake. What has Frances got to say about it? (*She moves to the desk*)

Gerry Not much. She is nervous, and with good reason.

Eva Don't be misled by that pleasant intellectual manner of hers. She is not as straightforward as she appears. She had an affair with Randolph once.

Gerry You knew about that?

Eva Oh yes, everyone did. They made little effort to hide it. She thought he was her passport to the top.

Gerry She has not done too badly.

Eva But not as far or as fast as she hoped.

Gerry I see.

Eva Watch her — that's all I'm saying.

Gerry I will.

Eva If it's not you or me or them, could it have been Turnbull?

Gerry Why not — he would have become the Prime Minister — quite an incentive.

Eva Randolph certainly didn't take his own life, and we still don't know who did. The same goes for Nigel. God knows why that was allowed to be hushed up.

Gerry We had enough on our plate at the time.

The buzzer goes, Gerry answers

(*Into the phone*) Yes, Melissa, show them up please.

Eva I suppose it's just possible Nigel could have died of natural causes. (*She shrugs. Going to the door*) Be careful, Gerry. These last weeks have been happy for me — I'd like us to go on for a bit longer.

Gerry So would I. I still wonder what it was Nigel had found out . . .

There is a knock on the hall door and Frances and Dick enter

Dick I was under the impression this was supposed to be a private meeting.

Eva It's all right, I'm just going. I look forward to see you later for dinner. You're always such fun.

Dick holds the door as Eva exits to the hall

Gerry Have you worked out a scheme so that I can retire gracefully and enjoy my ill-gotten gains?

Dick (*going over to the desk*) I feel we should watch what we say. The place may be bugged.

Gerry Don't worry. Security checks regularly — and unlike Nixon I don't keep tapes. They are likely to be used against you. Frances, you're looking worried.

Frances (*serious*) I've not been sleeping well recently. What we are doing is treason.

Gerry When you planned it, what did you think it was?

Frances What we did, the course of action we took was selfish in the extreme — but I could justify it to myself on the grounds of expediency. (*She sits in the chair* R *of the desk*)

Dick (*firmly*) But it was only meant to be for a very short time. Now the situation is getting out of hand. You are making decisions without consultation. You seem to believe you *are* the Prime Minister. (*He sits* L *of the table*)

Gerry A good actor has to believe in the part. So what do you suggest?

Frances We've considered various possibilities . . . (*She ticks off points on her finger*) One — you would disappear. Two — you would resign and retire. Three——

Gerry I could die.

Dick and Frances look uncomfortable

Or do a deal with the Secret Service.

Dick (*reluctantly agreeing*) Which I am afraid they are only too willing to do these days.

Gerry (*going to the drinks cabinet*) So we'd better all enjoy it while it lasts. Your usual? (*He pours drinks*) How are you getting on with the hornets' nest you've undertaken, Dick? It's been the graveyard of many politicians. (*He hands out the drinks*)

Dick (*deadly serious*) It will be the springboard to the summit of my ambitions. I *know* I can succeed where others failed.

Frances looks at him in astonishment

Frances I hadn't realized you felt like that. I presumed you were furious at getting the job.

Dick (*pulling himself together, lightly*) Oh, I was. But then I began to think about it and realized that the more difficult the problem, the greater the success.

Gerry . Bravo! What a team I have. You'd better get a move on though, with Ray Turnbull as Chancellor of the Exchequer it won't be too long before the country goes bust.

Frances (*laughing*) I hope that was a wise move.

Gerry It was a pragmatic decision. We have to keep him happy. Don't those chaps from the Treasury do all the sums? He can't do worse than the last four Chancellors. (*He raises his glass*) Here's to us. Long may we reign!

The red phone rings

If that's the President I made the fatal mistake of congratulating him on his microphone technique — now he tries out his speeches on me. (*He picks up the receiver*) Hello. . . . Put him through. . . . *Oui, Monsieur le Président. Bon soir. . . . Une excellente idée. . . . D'accord.* My staff will work out an agenda. . . . Agenda, it's Latin. *Dans deux semaines, alors. . . . Bon. Au revoir.* (*He replaces the receiver*) *Merde!*

Dick (*sarcastically*) Amuse yourself by all means, Jackson, but don't forget that desk is only on loan. (*He stands and moves upstage to the door to the hall. He opens the door, takes a pace back into the room and stands transfixed*)

Colonel Hardacre enters

W — what the hell?

The retiring room door opens and Turnbull enters

Colonel I'm sorry to sound melodramatic — but would you sit down, Mr Marr?

Dick sits

And nobody move. (*He moves to the desk*)

Gerry Ray! What on earth is going on?

Turnbull You'll find out very shortly, Mr Jackson — that is your name, I believe. Or are you going to deny it?

Gerry Jackson?! What are you talking about.

Turnbull (*crossing upstage to the desk*) Gerald Jackson. Actor. Flat forty-six Hartley Wood Mansions, Pimlico. Your agent's name is Julian Norton. Your bank is Barclays and you were married and divorced from Patricia Palmer, a former dancer. Now can we dispense with any displays of innocence — however well portrayed?

Dick (*rising*) This is incredible! Are you suggesting this is *not* Randolph Bolton? (*He sits in the chair* R *of the table*)

Turnbull The same goes for you, Marr — and anyway you haven't got Jackson's technique.

*Dick subsides and glares at Turnbull. Frances who is obviously terrified tries to
say something*

Frances Surely you don't imagine that I am a party to——
Turnbull (*bored*) Do shut up, Frances. Now, Mr Jackson.
Gerry (*shrugging and smiling*) If you are so sure—just what was that happy
little chat about, that we were having earlier?
Turnbull There were a few things that have been worrying me about you—I
needed to be certain.
Gerry What things?
Turnbull There never was a drunken dinner at the *Saracen's Head*, for one
thing.
Gerry (*nodding*) I was worried about that . . .
Turnbull Randolph Bolton never had a sense of humour and there were a few
matters he was intransigent about—one of them was Northern Ireland. He
would never have countenanced the steps Marr is taking.
Gerry Those are not concrete facts.
Turnbull I have to give credit to our usually much maligned Security
Services. Colonel Hardacre is mainly responsible. He's done an excellent
job.
Colonel But there were one or two matters, Mr Turnbull, that I wanted to
clarify before the whole thing became too public.
Frances But we only intended using Gerry Jackson to get us through the
election.
Turnbull (*surprised*) So you admit that?

She nods

Dick It was all her idea.
Colonel Which you just went along with, Marr?
Dick Well . . . yes.
Gerry (*interested*) Do tell me how you found out, Colonel?
Colonel (*hesitating*) Mr Turnbull?
Turnbull Go ahead, Hardacre. I shall enjoy this.
Colonel When I analysed the contents of the rum bottle I found no poison
but I did find two main sets of fingerprints—the Prime Minister's, which
we verified with the computer, and another. In collecting various prints
from other people in the household—surreptitiously, of course . . .
Gerry (*drily*) Of course.
Colonel We discovered that—(*pause while he enjoys the dramatic effect*)—
your prints were *not* the Prime Minister's.
Gerry (*still easy*) That must have confused you.
Colonel Well let's say it started the machinery in motion. You were quite
right that we checked the room regularly for bugging devices. We were
installing them.
Dick (*grimly*) I told you not to be careless.
Gerry It was getting so tiring, endlessly taking walks. I must know every tree
in St James's Park by now. They are probably bugged as well. And I have
to admit that as no-one appeared at all suspicious—it seemed an

unnecessary precaution. (*Brightly*) Well how long am I going to get for impersonating a Prime Minister?

Turnbull It is nothing like that simple as you well know, Jackson.

Gerry (*surprised*) Do I?

Colonel We took some time to find out your identity—you have no criminal record and appeared in none of our computer print-outs. But, of course we eventually tracked you down and then thoroughly researched your background and activities.

Gerry Tell me how you found out.

Colonel I won't go into details—but perhaps it was unwise of you to be signed in on your first visit under your real name.

Gerry Oh yes, of course.

Colonel Over the last two years, since you worked in that repertory company in Lincolnshire, you have not acted at all.

Gerry Er ... no, it has been a bad patch.

Colonel And yet during that time your life-style improved. Not too obviously of course, but in subtle ways; a new small car, some expensive clothes, a couple of pairs of hand-made shoes and three trips abroad to Switzerland.

Gerry I like skiing—I came into money ... a relative died.

Colonel Not true and easily checked. Those trips were part of your detailed briefings.

Gerry Briefings?

Frances What is all this leading up to?

Turnbull You'll find out soon. (*He moves upstage behind the desk*) The Colonel did a thorough job. Having learnt who the conspirators were he decided to research all of you—in depth. He wanted all the facts and he suspected, correctly, that the death of Randolph Bolton was a planned, deliberate, political assassination.

Gerry (*starting to rise*) I had nothing to do with that! I thought I was working for the Home Office. I thought I was one of the good guys.

Colonel Sit down, Mr Jackson.

Gerry subsides

Mrs Cowdray, you appear to have acted on impulse. We cannot find anything to suggest otherwise ... at the moment. Your crimes were the usual ones of ambition and vanity.

Frances I cannot deny that ... I was very foolish. But I don't under-stand——

Turnbull You will, if you listen instead of talking for a change. Carry on, Colonel.

Colonel We started with Eva Bolton—she appeared to be the most obvious suspect as ...

Dick (*who has been listening intently*) Are you *sure* that you've got your facts right, Hardacre? Turnbull is the man you should be investigating.

Colonel We did, thoroughly, but we have compiled a far more interesting dossier on you. The more we looked the more it grew.

Dick I feel it is time we were all legally represented (*to Frances and Gerry*) and I insist that neither of you say another word.

Colonel I am not asking them to at the moment, Mr Marr. I am just explaining some interesting facts that have come to light. Among your various activities you have taken many trips abroad.

Dick (*sarcastically*) As a Cabinet Minister that is hardly surprising.

Colonel Several of those trips were on official business. But it is the unofficial contacts whom you met that have proved so interesting.

Dick Really?

Colonel (*moving behind Dick*) You took holidays in Switzerland, and apart from the regular visits to your (*acidly*) numbered bank accounts, these visits, in the last two years, have coincided with Mr Jackson's trips.

Frances (*incredulous*) Do you mean you've been working on this for two years?

Gerry Yes, Frances. I'm sorry to disillusion you. I am a quick learner and I *am* good at ad-libbing, but I've been studying this part for *many* months.

Frances is stunned

That's why (*modestly*) I'm so good at it.

Frances But it was my idea. I was the one who thought of you.

Colonel I think you'll find you were carefully led into it. Doubtless if you had not come up with the suggestion, Mr Marr would have done. After you told him about Jackson, he checked up and recruited him.

Frances But I would have known . . . (*She hesitates*)

Dick (*angrily, standing and moving upstage*) You are all going to look very foolish when this becomes public knowledge. Perhaps it is time to put our cards on the table. (*He is apparently confident*) What's the deal? To start with I presume we have to resign . . .

Turnbull (*quietly*) No deal.

Dick Oh, come on, there *has* to be a deal of some sort. If the great British public even suspected they had been governed by an out-of-work actor they would never trust Parliament again.

Colonel (*aside*) It hasn't worried the Americans too much.

Turnbull (*grimly*) There is not going to be any arrangement or accommodation or deal. If the matter was as simple as you would like us to believe it might have been possible; but in view of your other activities . . . (*He stops and shrugs*)

Dick What do you mean? I was just thinking of winning the election.

Colonel Primarily your connection with a foreign government and a political terrorist organization.

Dick This is preposterous. I absolutely deny the charge.

Colonel (*reasonably*) We usually assume that the great threat to us comes from Russia and the Eastern Bloc. Certainly they have proved embarrassingly efficient at infiltrating our security services. They are far-sighted in the use of "sleepers" who lie dormant for many years before they are useful. You are a "sleeper", Mr Marr.

Dick (*confidently, moving upstage to face the Colonel*) I have no connection with Russia. You are just throwing around wild and unsubstantiated allegations. As usual M.I.5 are making fools of themselves.

Colonel I admit our assumption did hold up our investigations for a little while until we realized your affiliation was never to Communism.

Dick What do you mean?

Colonel We now have everything we need ... to prove you have been an officer in the Irish Republican Army for over twenty-five years.

Gerry ⎫
Frances ⎭ *(together)* ⎰ Good God!
⎱ *(standing and moving upstage)* It can't be true!

Colonel Before you went to Cambridge, in fact.

Dick Prove it!

Colonel In a raid just before dawn this morning, my men arrested three members of an IRA active service unit here in London—Camden Town to be precise. A fourth man was shot dead and one of the prisoners is wounded, but he has been "helping us with our enquiries".

Turnbull And has proved most co-operative.

Dick I don't believe you.

Colonel It is unusual—but then he somehow got the idea that *you* had betrayed them.

Dick You bastards. (*He turns and faces them. Bitterly*) What stupid fools you are. Don't you realize that if you let me get on with my job I would have done this country the greatest service.

Turnbull By helping Northern Ireland to become part of the Republic, I suppose.

Dick Exactly! Do you honestly think the average English, Scot or Welshman cares a damn about Ulster? They would be happy to see the whole expensive, bloody island towed out into the Atlantic and sunk.

Frances What are you talking about? You are a traitor.

Dick Traitor? What an emotive word ... and traitor to whom? What you and your complacent colleagues lack is any political idealism. You're the traitors, you are only activated by self interest.

Frances (*spirited*) And you aren't? You'd do anything for power.

Dick Yes—but not for me—for the cause. (*He moves towards the door*) And *you*, you're a classic example, Frances. You have no standards at all. They say politics makes strange bed-fellows—but (*with great contempt*) Randolph Bolton!

Frances is mortified

Colonel Don't move any further, Marr. (*He takes out a gun fitted with a silencer from the inside of his coat*)

Dick I'm not taking any orders from you. (*He moves to the hall door and opens it*)

Colonel (*icily*) I'll shoot if I have to.

Dick Why should that matter to me; a hero's death is better than a lifetime in prison.

Gerry (*finding his voice*) You'll be unsung, the gesture will be pointless.

Turnbull Stay out of it, Jackson—it's nothing to do with you.

Gerry It has everything to do with me. You *want* him dead, don't you? . . .
Dick — were you personally responsible for the death of Bolton?
Dick Yes.
Gerry And Nigel?
Dick Yes. Randolph's little lap dog had to be put down. He was sniffing
around a little too close to the truth. (*He turns to go*)
Colonel Don't move!
Dick If you use that you'll bring the whole system down. Right?
Colonel I mean it.

*Dick starts to leave. The Colonel fires with his silenced gun. Dick is hit into the
doorway*

Dick I . . . didn't . . . (*He dies and falls outside the door*)

The Colonel moves into the hallway and stoops over the body

Eva appears in the doorway

Colonel Mrs Bolton, stay outside, please.
Eva No, Colonel Hardacre. (*She enters the room and goes to Gerry*) Are you
all right?
Gerry Yes, yes. As they used to say in the movies — the game is up.
Colonel (*to an off-stage character*) All right, Robinson — wait here, I'll call
you in a moment.

The Colonel enters the room and closes the door

Eva Did you have to kill him?
Colonel (*abruptly*) Yes.

Eva shakes her head in disbelief and looks at Turnbull

Turnbull (*coldly*) There mustn't be any loose ends. It's tidier this way.
Eva What happens now?
Frances The Colonel has just created a new martyr.
Colonel I don't think so — you see this incident never occurred.
Frances But we all saw——
Turnbull (*harshly*) Nothing!
Colonel Marr will have no soldier's death — he will have an unfortunate car
accident — probably in the company of the Prime Minister. Doubtless the
car will burst into flames.

Pause

Gerry (*moving downstage to face the Colonel*) Ah! . . . I don't want to appear
naïve but may I enquire what you will use for the PM's body?
Turnbull That depends.
Gerry On what?
Turnbull On how the three of you co-operate.
Gerry Oh, I'll co-operate, I assure you.
Frances So will I.
Eva Don't worry, they can't shoot all of us.

Gerry (*doubtfully*) Can't they? I'm beginning to wonder.
Eva I think you'll find that Gerry has taken some precautions to safeguard his position.

Gerry is not quite sure what she means but manages to look significant

Turnbull Don't try and bluff me, Eva, your participation has been most unsavoury.
Eva I had my reasons (*she looks at Gerry*) and one of them was personal.
Gerry Thank you, darling.
Turnbull Loyalty to your husband might have got my sympathy but your behaviour with this imposter was treasonable.
Eva My only treason was to keep quiet about Randolph for so many years. He was completely corrupt. He hurt everybody near him and he could be very cruel. At least our acting Prime Minister is kind.
Turnbull You've all behaved in a despicable way.
Eva Your righteous indignation is most impressive, Ray. Are you sure there aren't one or two skeletons in your cupboard? (*She glances at Gerry*)
Turnbull Certainly not!
Gerry (*drily*) Nobody is what they seem.
Frances I suppose you *are* Scotland Yard, Colonel Hardacre—or M.I.5 or something?
Turnbull That is one thing I have checked up on. (*To Colonel Hardacre*) How long have you known about Jackson?
Colonel For two weeks.
Turnbull (*furiously*) And you let him stay on as Prime Minister?
Frances (*almost to herself*) He did less harm than most.
Eva He has done a very good job. He is not an evil man, it is just that he sees life in terms of a film script.

Gerry nods ruefully

Turnbull Well now the time has come for him to pay the penalty for his action. And you as well, Frances.
Frances But I——
Eva (*firmly*) That would be a mistake, I think, Ray.
Turnbull What do you mean?
Eva Do you intend to put them on trial—in an open court?
Turnbull Colonel?

Turnbull looks enquiringly at Hardacre who shrugs and moves back to the door

Colonel My job is security, Chancellor. You have to make the political decisions. If you'll excuse me I must go and deal with my men. Before making your decision perhaps there is something you should know.
Turnbull Yes, Colonel?
Colonel It concerns Mrs Bolton.
Eva No, Colonel Hardacre. It isn't necessary.
Turnbull Go ahead, Hardacre.
Eva Please, Colonel . . .

Colonel You should know that for the last two years Mrs Bolton has been working for my department.

Turnbull (*after a pause*) Working for you?

Frances Is there anyone here who hasn't been working on this for two years?

Colonel It was considered necessary once when the Prime Minister made several unexplained trips to Moscow.

Turnbull You mean she was spying on her own husband?

The Colonel nods; Eva looks at Gerry

Gerry You really are a sleeper, aren't you?

Eva I'm sorry, Gerry, I hoped you'd never have to know. It had nothing to do with us. I wanted to tell you but of course I couldn't.

Turnbull Why was I not informed of Mrs Bolton's position earlier?

Colonel I could hardly tell you, sir—you were a suspect.

Turnbull (*deflated*) I see.

Colonel I'll be outside if you want me. I leave you to make the decision, Chancellor.

The Colonel exits to the hall

Eva I'm sorry, Gerry.

Gerry There seems to be more acting going on in Downing Street than at the National Theatre.

Frances Well, Ray, what are you going to do?

Turnbull I don't have any choice.

Eva Yes you do. If this whole thing comes out in the open you won't be able to cover up Marr's death to start with.

Turnbull There could be a way . . .

Eva No way. *All* the facts will have to come out—including some embarrassing revelations from the past. Embarrassing for you, that is.

Gerry understands what she means—at last . . .

Turnbull (*less sure of himself*) I have nothing to hide.

Eva Not even Ultrasonic Marine Investments?

Turnbull (*visibly taken aback*) Ultrasonic—what has that to do with it?

Gerry We have all the details, from Randolph's private file.

Turnbull (*subdued*) I see.

Gerry It would seem a great pity if you and your brother-in-law had to lose those lucrative consultancies.

The red phone rings. Gerry picks up his glass and walks away. They all hesitate then Turnbull answers

Turnbull Yes? . . . No, this is the Chancellor of the Exchequer, but put him on. Ray Turnbull here, Mr President. Can I do anything for you? . . . I see. . . . Yes, he has been very busy. . . . You particularly want him *now*. . . . Well I'll see if I can get him to the phone—would you mind holding for a minute. . . . (*He covers the mouthpiece and hesitates as he looks at the others*) It appears that you have established a very special relationship with the President. He's very insistent on talking to the PM (*He pauses*) On thinking things over it is probably sensible for us to handle the whole "incident" with discretion.

Eva Oh Ray, you're so sensitive, you're wasted in politics.

Turnbull It will give us time to organize the circumstances of Randolph's demise at a more appropriate moment.

Frances After all we can't get any more bodies under the bed.

Turnbull Yes. Well, you'd better take your call. I have to admit you are doing an excellent job, Prime Minister.

Gerry moves to the desk, sits in the chair and picks up the telephone receiver

Gerry Randolph here—hi. ... You have to address an international convention of bankers? ... No, no, please go ahead, I'd love to hear your speech.

CURTAIN

FURNITURE AND PROPERTY LIST

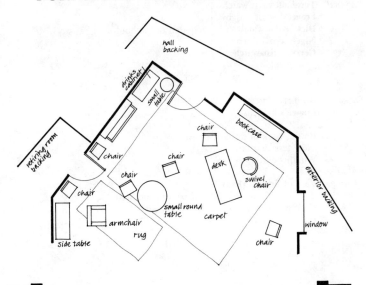

ACT I

SCENE 1

On stage: Desk. *On it:* red telephone, white intercom telephone, black external telephone, blotter, papers, pens, pencils. *In drawer:* papers, copy of Official Secrets Act

Swivel chair

Bookcase unit. *On shelves:* books, telephone directories

Window curtains (closed)

Chair by window

Small round table

3 chairs

Drinks cabinet. *In it:* bottles of drink including rum, brandy, Scotch, tonic, jug of water, glasses

Small table. *On it:* table lamp

Fireplace with mantelpiece and club fender

Armchair

2 chairs

Side table. *On it:* table lamp

Carpet

Rug

Off stage: Wallet and keys **(Frances)**
    Shoe **(Gerry)**
    Briefcase **(Frances)**
    Briefcase **(Dick)**
    Briefcase. *In it:* address book **(Turnbull)**
    Papers **(Nigel)**

Personal: **Turnbull:** wrist-watch
    Frances: wrist-watch
    Dick: wrist-watch } required throughout
    Nigel: wrist-watch
    Gerry: wrist-watch

SCENE 2

Strike: All dirty glasses
   France's briefcase

Set: Bottles back in drinks cabinet
   Tidy desk and table
   Window curtains open

Off stage: Vase of flowers **(Eva)**
    Briefcase containing sheet of paper **(Turnbull)**
    Correspondence book and letters **(Nigel)**
    Briefcase **(Hardacre)**

ACT II

SCENE 1

Check: **Hardacre's** briefcase.

Personal: **Hardacre:** handkerchief
    Gerry: keys in pocket
    Nigel: envelope in pocket

SCENE 2

Strike: Dirty glass, envelope, paper from desk
   Vase of flowers from table
   Gerry's jacket

Set: Open folder with letter on desk
   Close desk drawer

Personal: **Hardacre:** gun with silencer in pocket

LIGHTING PLOT

Practical fittings required: pendant above desk, 2 table lamps
Interior. A study. The same scene throughout

ACT I, Scene 1   Night
To open: All practicals on; hall lit, retiring room lit

No cues

ACT I, Scene 2   Late afternoon

To open: General interior lighting; hall lit, retiring room lit

Cue 1   **Nigel** switches on main light   (Page 26)
       Snap on pendant

ACT II, Scene 1   Evening

To open: As end Act I, Scene 2

Cue 2   **Nigel** reads paper from desk drawer; hand switches off main   (Page 42)
       light
       Snap off pendant

Cue 3   **Gerry** switches on main light   (Page 42)
       Snap on pendant

ACT II, Scene 2   Evening

To open: All practicals on; hall lit, retiring room lit

No cues

EFFECTS PLOT

ACT I

Cue 1   **Frances** and **Dick** drag body into retiring room   (Page 8)
Intercom phone buzzes

Cue 2   **Frances** appears at retiring room door   (Page 8)
Intercom phone buzzes

Cue 3   **Frances** and **Dick** exit to retiring room   (Page 12)
Intercom phone buzzes; pause, then buzz again

Cue 4   **Dick** and **Gerry** exit to retiring room   (Page 15)
Pause, then red phone rings

Cue 5   **Frances:** "... by Colonel Hardacre."   (Page 18)
Intercom phone buzzes

Cue 6   **Gerry:** "... I thought you would."   (Page 29)
Intercom phone buzzes

Cue 7   **Eva** sits in chair by window   (Page 31)
Intercom phone buzzes

Cue 8   **Turnbull:** "... paper was confidential."   (Page 32)
Intercom phone buzzes

ACT II

Cue 9   **Dick:** "Right, that's agreed."   (Page 40)
Intercom phone buzzes

Cue 10   **Gerry:** "... our plate at the time."   (Page 46)
Intercom phone buzzes

Cue 11   **Gerry:** "Long may we reign!"   (Page 48)
Red phone rings

Cue 12   **Colonel** fires gun at **Dick**   (Page 53)
Silenced gunshot

Cue 13   **Gerry:** "... those lucrative consultancies."   (Page 55)
Red phone rings

MADE AND PRINTED IN GREAT BRITAIN BY
LATIMER TREND & COMPANY LTD PLYMOUTH

MADE IN ENGLAND